The Problem Pony Book

The Problem Pony Book

Carolyn Henderson

and

Lynn Russell

J. A. Allen
London

British Library Cataloguing-in-Publication Data.
A catalogue record for this book is available from the British Library

ISBN 0.85131.620.4

Published in Great Britain in 1995 by
J. A. Allen & Company Limited,
1 Lower Grosvenor Place, Buckingham Palace Road,
London, SW1W 0EL

Typeset by Textype Typesetters, Cambridge
Printed by Dah Hua Printing Press Co., Hong Kong

Illustrations by Ann Pilgrim
Designed by Nancy Lawrence
Photographs by John Henderson

Contents

Acknowledgements

Thanks to our models, Terry Mansfield and Kitty (who is not a problem pony but posed beautifully as one) and Anna Thorogood and Clover, and to Charles Owen for supplying the hats.

Life would be much simpler if your pony could read this book

Introduction

Keeping and riding ponies is a series of challenges. Some are enjoyable, some are frustrating and some can be worrying – even frightening. Because you are dealing with an animal rather than a machine, you cannot guarantee that if you press the right button you will always get the right reaction. Nine times out of ten you will, but now and then things go wrong.

No matter how good a rider you are, there are bound to be times when you have problems. It may be something minor, such as the pony not wanting to open his mouth for the bit, or it may be a serious and potentially dangerous problem, such as rearing. Nearly all problems can be solved through correct handling and riding, although sometimes you have to be even cleverer and more determined than your pony.

Life would be much easier if you could present your pony with this book and suggest he reads the appropriate section; it could save you both a lot of time, trouble and perhaps discomfort! Having said that, there are still some ponies who would probably blow a raspberry at you and carry on regardless.

Problem ponies can be very demoralising. There are times when they make you feel stupid, incompetent and not fit to be in charge of a well-behaved hamster. Ponies can reduce you to tears of frustration and howls of rage with surprising ease!

Your pony will undoubtedly be part of the family. Even if you are the only person who rides him, others are bound to become involved with him. Inevitably, they will be as concerned as you are if you hit a problem and will want to try to help you find a solution.

For that reason, this book is designed to be a family reference book. It is neither safe nor sensible to try to tackle problems on your own; sometimes all you will need is another pair of hands but there may also be occasions when you need specialist advice and expertise, perhaps from your instructor or farrier.

Everyone has problems at some time, even if they have so many years of experience that they probably wore nappies under their jodhpurs. Remember that the problems that arise are not always your fault: most are caused by bad handling or riding somewhere along the line . . . but the origin of the problem you encounter today may go back much further. Previous owners can also have selective memories: it is not unusual to be told that Dobbin 'never did that when we had him' only to learn from someone else that he was actually quite well known for it.

Most problems can be solved as long as you remember a few golden rules. The first is that no matter what you are trying to put right, your own safety must always be top priority. This means never taking unnecessary risks and always taking sensible precautions, such as wearing BSI-standard headgear, protective footwear and gloves when necessary. Accidents do not always happen when horses are being ridden: if a pony you are trying to load into a trailer rears and comes down on your head or your foot, you will be very glad of your hat or your boots with steel toecaps!

Safety considerations often bring in the second rule – get help from an experienced adult who is used to dealing with ponies. This can be anyone from other members of your family (provided they have the necessary knowledge) to your riding instructor. Reputable dealers and people who break and school horses for a living can also be good contacts as they have usually found out, through trial and error, how to sort out problem animals.

Never be ashamed of asking for help. Knowledgeable people will respect you for it because they will recognise that you are putting your pony's welfare first. Small problems that go unsolved grow into big ones, and the more established a bad habit becomes, the harder it is to break.

Ponies are creatures of instinct. No matter how well schooled or worldly wise they are, they will always follow the same basic behaviour patterns. Recognising these – learning how to think like a horse – will make you a better owner and rider and give you a headstart on coping with problems as soon as they arise.

In the wild, horses are prey animals rather than predators. If they are attacked, their natural defence is to turn and run rather than stand and fight. So if anything frightens them, they instinctively want to get away from it as quickly as possible.

They are also herd animals and so like company. If a pony has plenty of human company, he may adapt to living alone for a while but he will always be happier if he has an equine companion. Failing this, he may make friends with another animal such as a goat; some highly strung Thoroughbred racehorses have sheep or goats as companions, which live in their stables and travel everywhere with them.

A horse's senses are much more finely tuned than a person's. His hearing has a far greater range and he has acute senses of smell and touch. This is why horses hate loud noises and like to investigate anything new or suspicious by sniffing at it.

Because a horse's eyes are set in the side of his head, he can see almost all round him. Most of the time, he turns his head so that he is using one eye to look at one thing while the other eye is looking at something else. This means that he can see much more than we can, but he is not as good at judging distances. It also explains why he dislikes sudden movements and why he needs the freedom of his head and neck to assess a jump and negotiate it successfully.

Opinions vary as to how intelligent horses and ponies are. Some people assume that they must be stupid to allow us to dominate and ride them, particularly when even the smallest pony is stronger than a big man. However, horses are used to being in a hierarchy. In any group of horses there is a pecking order, starting with the boss horse at the top and moving down the line to the most subservient.

You need to be higher than your pony in the pecking order if your relationship is to work. This does not mean that he must be frightened of you but, rather, that he accepts what you tell him (most of the time, at least!). There is only one way to achieve this and that is by firm, kind and consistent handling.

Horses learn by repetition. In the simplest terms, your pony should know that when you close your legs on his sides, it is an instruction to go forwards. If you change the signal, he will not understand. He will also be confused if you carry on giving a signal after he has obeyed it, as we shall see later in the riding section.

It is vital that you are consistent. If you laugh at your pony for bucking one day when you are in a good mood, and hit him the next because you feel fed up, he will not know whether his behaviour is acceptable.

Our relationship with horses is based on a system of reward and punishment which, luckily, is not as unpleasant as it sounds. Reward does not always mean stuffing him with titbits, any more than punishment means hitting him.

Rewarding a pony can be anything from stopping giving an aid because he has done what you asked him to, to praising him with your voice or a pat on the neck. In the same way, punishment could be repeating an aid, more strongly this time, using your voice sharply or hitting him. It is important to stay calm when you punish a pony and to try not to lose your temper – if you blow your top you will only make things worse.

Rewards and punishments must follow on immediately from whatever prompted them. It is no good smacking a pony a minute after he has bitten you because he will not put the two actions together. Similarly, while it might make you feel nice to give him extra carrots when you get home from a successful show, your pony will not realise why he is getting them.

It is natural to want to be friends with your pony, but friendship should never mean letting good manners fly out of the door. Ponies are working animals who must be treated with respect as well as affection – it is too easy to get hurt by one who has no respect for his handlers. This is especially true of small ponies; they may look cute enough to have stepped straight out of a Thelwell cartoon but they should be treated as proper horses, not cuddly pets.

Some problems can be dealt with quickly and simply once you know the right techniques. Others take longer to solve, perhaps because there is more than one underlying cause or because the obvious approach simply does not work. You often have to work out why a pony behaves in a certain way before you can start putting things right: perhaps he has lost his confidence about jumping because a previous rider asked him to tackle fences that were beyond his training or ability, or perhaps he is tense because his tack does not fit and is causing him discomfort or even pain.

Whatever problem you are tackling, there is a shortlist of questions to ask:

- Does the pony understand what he is being asked to do?
- Is he frightened?
- Is something causing him pain or discomfort?
- If so, what is it and how can it be put right – for instance, do his teeth have sharp edges that need rasping or is his saddle pinching?
- Is he being fed too much high-energy food?

Problems are rarely solved overnight unless they are the kind that can be nipped in the bud. For example, most youngsters go through a stage of feeling very clever and may suddenly decide that perhaps they do not have to do all that you ask of them after all. This is when quick, decisive action (such as a hard smack on the girth when he decides he does not want to go past his own gate) can work wonders.

In many cases, you are faced with lines of communication that have broken down and it is your job to open them up again. This may involve going right back to basics and it will frequently mean that you have to look at your own riding and handling skills.

Most problems can be solved through a combination of patience, skill and 'pony psychology'. If a particular problem proves insurmountable, however, the only sensible course of action is to find the pony another home, doing another job, where he will be happier: for instance, a reluctant jumper may make a lovely hack or even turn his hoof to dressage.

What you have to decide is whether the buck stops here (no pun intended) or is passed on. In other words, you either seek help to sort out the problem or − if it turns out to be something that cannot be cured and makes the pony unsuitable for your circumstances − get rid of him.

If it comes to selling, you must be honest about it (which may seem hard if someone has pulled the wool over your eyes). However, think how you would feel if you sold a pony with a serious problem, such as rearing, and you later discovered that a child had been injured, or worse, because of him.

In this situation there is only one answer that will allow you an easy conscience. The pony must be sold to a professional and you must make it clear that the problem exists − even if you lose money. It is even worth insisting that the purchaser signs an agreement stating that he or she has been told that the pony rears, is unreliable in traffic or whatever.

Some people may suggest that you enter the pony in a sale, unwarranted. This means that you make no guarantee as to his behaviour or soundness and anyone bidding for him knowingly takes that risk. The problem is that if you do this, you do not know where the pony will finish up. He may be lucky and end up in the hands of someone who can sort him out, but there is an equal chance that he will go through a lot of hands very quickly and end up with the meatman (perhaps injuring someone on his way there).

If you cannot sell a pony with a dangerous problem to someone experienced enough to solve it, you may have to consider having him put down. This is the worst possible scenario and, with luck, one that you will not have to cope with − even if there are times when you feel like wringing his neck because you can't catch him/load him into the trailer/get him to go through water!

We make no apologies for what may seem like repetitive advice throughout this book because so often problems come down to basics − such as teeth that need rasping (the pony's rather than the owner grinding his or hers through frustration!), incorrectly fitted tack or over-feeding/feeding the wrong sort of food. *Whatever the problem, always check these basics first.*

If you enjoy riding and looking after ponies, then, by definition, you are the sort of person who enjoys meeting challenges. Few things give greater satisfaction than overcoming a schooling or handling problem and going on to the next stage in your and your pony's progress.

This book is designed to help to solve most of the problems you will come across. The methods in it (both the orthodox and the more unusual ones) have been tried and proven with the help of a variety of horses and ponies of all ages. Prevention is definitely better than cure but it is never too late to improve a pony's manners or schooling.

The book is divided into three sections and the problems are listed in alphabetical order. The first section is on handling ponies, the second covers riding and schooling problems, and the final one deals with common health worries – starting with a guide to recognising when things are wrong and when you should call the vet.

Most of us ride and keep ponies for pleasure and there is no enjoyment to be had with an animal that is ignorant or bad mannered. The most ordinary pony can give you a lot of fun if he is pleasant, obedient and well schooled. That is what this book is about – helping you to find the answers to your problems so that you and your pony can enjoy life together.

Handling and Leading

Barging

Ponies who barge and throw their weight about, either in the stable or when you are leading them, have to be taught the error of their ways. Luckily, you do not need strength to do this: the secret lies in technique.

With the pony who barges in his box, walk up to the door with a short stick in your hand. Do not rush in waving the stick about: bang the door with it so that he steps back from the noise. If, when you open the door, he tries to rush towards you, go in and hit him a single sharp blow across the chest – no higher, or you might make him headshy.

At the same time, use your voice. This is one of the most important aids and is often forgotten. Say 'No!' in a sharp tone and he will soon associate this with disapproval. When he obeys, talk to him and praise him in a soft voice.

If he tries to barge while you are leading him, make sure that you are equipped with maximum control and safety. A stroppy pony who jumps on

The right equipment can help prevent injury

When handling or riding a difficult pony, always wear a hard hat

Clipping the leadrope so that it acts as a 'curb chain' and gives extra control over a pony who tries to barge off when you lead him. The smooth side of the clip must be next to the pony's face so that it cannot dig in

your foot, tries to pull a lead rein through your hand or leaps up in the air and catches you as he comes down can cause a lot of painful damage. Gloves, boots with blocked-in toes and a hard hat or skull cap give you a better fighting chance.

Put a bridle on the pony, not a headcollar, and, if possible, use a lead rein with a chain section near the clip end. If you are leading so that the pony is on your right, clip the lead rein to the right-hand bit ring and pass it under the chin and through the other bit ring. This will provide an extra control point by putting pressure on the curb groove. If you do not have a chain lead rein, use your ordinary reins: unbuckle the reins and pass the right one under the chin and through the left bit ring as before.

Hold the rein in your inside hand and a short stick in your outside one. If the pony tries to rush off, give a sharp tug on the rein and smack him once across the chest. There should be a sharp, but by no means violent, 'take and give' on the rein; a steady pull will do no good at all and will only give him something to pull against.

At the same time, use your voice sharply: 'No' or 'Whoa' is usually effective, even if you feel like using something much stronger. It is not so much a matter of what you say as the way you say it! Practise leading the pony out but only hit him if he barges. When the message sinks home and he starts to walk sensibly, praise him and make a fuss of him.

Some ponies often barge on their way to the field because they are anxious to get out. Put on his headcollar and leadrope and put a bridle over the top, with the noseband removed for ease of handling and a curb-groove lead rein as before. When you have made him walk sensibly to the field, using our earlier tactics, slip off the bridle. In extreme cases, a Chifney bit used over the headcollar may give you even more control (see the section on loading).

The headcollar and leadrope should give you enough control to make sure that he goes off when you allow him to, not when he wants to. Turn his head towards the gate and step back as soon as you let him go. Then, if he does kick up his heels and gallop off, there is less risk of you getting kicked. If you make a habit of giving a small titbit after you have removed the headcollar, you will probably find that he stands and waits for this rather than galloping off.

Barging is a problem that can usually be cured quite quickly. However, if you are going to take your pony somewhere where he might get excited, it is always best to lead him in a bridle. There are special headcollars which are designed to give extra control, usually through a noseband that pulls tight when the pony pulls and loosens when he comes back to the handler, but these are not as effective as a bridle.

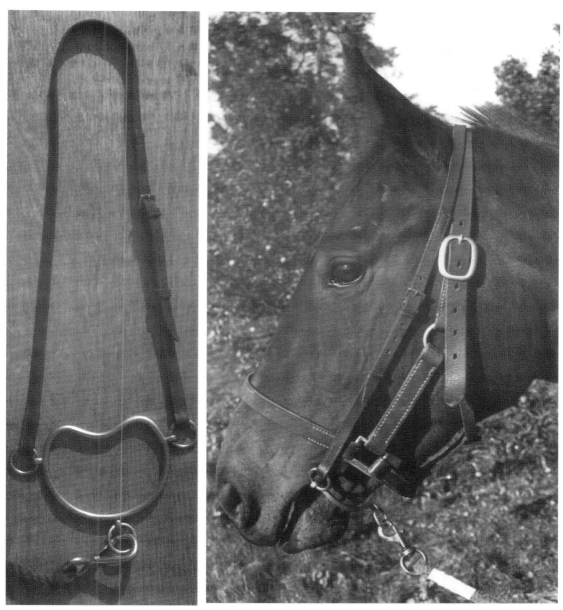

A Chifney bit gives maximum control when leading and is useful for ponies who are difficult to load

Biting

Biting is more often a reaction to actual (or anticipated) pain or discomfort rather than downright aggression. That does not make it any the less annoying or painful for whoever is at the sharp end but it does mean that you should check and, if necessary, modify the way you groom or tack up your pony. Well-bred animals with a high percentage of Thoroughbred blood usually have thinner skins and are more sensitive than native ponies, although even they have limits to their tolerance. (See the grooming and saddling sections for ways of coping.)

The simplest way of dealing with a biter is to tie him up as soon as you go into the stable. You can then groom, tack up or adjust rugs in safety (providing, of course, he does not kick as well! If he is that versatile, read the section on kicking.)

If you do not want to tie him up, put a snaffle bridle on him and take the reins over his head as if you were going to lead him. Put the reins over to the offside and then bring them over the neck, back to your hand. Hold them

Sometimes a pony will refuse to accept the bit

Hold the reins this way to prevent a pony from swinging his head round to bite you

normally while you do whatever job is necessary and, as soon as the pony attempts to bite you, apply a firm 'take and give'.

At the same time, use your voice. A sharp 'Oy' or 'No', coupled with a jerk on the reins, will soon let him know that biting will not be tolerated.

A sharp and immediate smack on the nose can deliver swift justice to a horse or pony that bites you as a 'one-off', but is not a good idea for the habitual offender. All that will probably happen is that you will make him headshy so that he bites and then throws his head up or jumps back to avoid the anticipated smack. Some people recommend that you react as another horse would and bite him back but this can also be a quick way of getting your teeth knocked out.

Bitting and Bridling

Ponies who are difficult to bridle or who object when you ask them to open their mouths and take the bit are either worried because they associate the procedure with pain – from sharp teeth or other mouth problems or previous rough handling – or plain naughty. Eliminate the question of mouth problems and check that your handling techniques are not to blame.

The best behaved pony will start to object if he is repeatedly banged on the teeth by a bit or if the bridle is removed carelessly or roughly and the mouthpiece catches on his teeth. Persuade him to open his mouth by pressing on the gap (where the bars are) at the side of his mouth with your fingers; tickling the tongue works in some cases. Be careful! The further you put your fingers in a horse's mouth, the more likely you are to get bitten.

The commonest evasion is for the pony to hold his head out of reach or throw it up. Do not try to find a way round this by standing on a bale or mounting block because this puts you in a very vulnerable position. If the pony throws up his head or barges at you, he may well send you flying.

Instead, fit a headcollar that buckles on the nose and at the side and then put on a saddle or roller. Fasten the leadrope between the front legs so that it acts like a standing martingale; it should be tight enough to prevent the pony from getting his head above the angle of control but not so tight that his head is tied between his knees. Then put on the bridle, gently and without force, and remove the headcollar when it is in place. Be patient and do not hit him or shout at him, which will only make things worse.

The same technique is useful for ponies that are reluctant to take the bit, because when they do open their mouths, they often throw up their heads at the same time. Remember that, for a young pony, suddenly being asked to have a foreign object in his mouth must be annoying or even frightening. Patience is the answer until he accepts it. You can also make the bit more acceptable by coating it in honey or molasses. Many youngsters find a hollow, lightweight mouthpiece or a Nathe bit with a flexible plastic mouthpiece easier to accept in the early stages than a heavy one.

If the pony dislikes having his ears touched, ask your vet to check for problems such as ear mites and see the section on being headshy. Sometimes a pony throws up his head to avoid his ears being touched and then bangs his muzzle on the bit: in this case, try removing the bit and put the bridle on as if it was a headcollar. When he accepts this, fasten the bit to the offside cheekpiece and press on the space (bars) between the teeth on the nearside of his lower jaw. As he opens his mouth, slide the bit in gently and fasten it to the nearside cheekpiece.

Box Walking

The box walker is like a tiger in its cage – he paces round and round his stable, which puts unwanted strain on his limbs and may make him more likely to throw splints (bony enlargements, usually found on the forelegs). This habit may also make it difficult to keep flesh on him. As with all stable vices (see crib biting, weaving and wind sucking sections), it is much more common in horses than ponies because most ponies are kept out most of the time and enjoy a reasonably natural lifestyle.

In the wild horses and ponies spend most of their time moving around and foraging for food. Keeping them shut up in stables most of the time is unnatural, so start by making sure that your pony has a more natural lifestyle. Turn him out, day and night if possible, well rugged up if necessary and with adequate shelter and he should behave more like a pony and less like a neurotic. The same prescription could be applied to a lot of horses.

If the box walker needs to be kept in part of the time, he will be better in a stall than a stable as long as he has other horses around him. Box walking is quite common in highly strung, super-fit Thoroughbred racehorses who are kept stabled most of the time and therefore live a lifestyle that is alien to their nature. Giving them a live-in companion, such as a goat or a sheep, seems to work with some, although this may not be possible if you keep your pony at livery.

Catching

Ponies that are difficult to catch waste both time and patience. They usually evade you because they associate being caught with something they would rather avoid – being ridden or being taken away from their grazing. What you have to do is set aside some time to persuade them that being caught can actually be the prelude to something enjoyable (food) and that work does not automatically follow on.

If possible, turn the offender out in a small area. No one enjoys trailing round ten acres after a pony who knows that all he has to do is trot away from you. If necessary, fence off a small area of your paddock with electric fencing (see escaping from a field for more information on setting this up).

The pony should be turned out with a leather headcollar on (an old one

Ponies that are hard to catch can be exasperating

serves the job well, rather than spoiling your best show headcollar). Never use a nylon headcollar unless it is one of the new designs with breakable rings. If the pony gets it caught up on something, leather will always break before he does himself any damage. With an ordinary nylon headcollar, it may be his neck that breaks first.

Make a loop of plaited baler twine large enough to clip a leadrope on to and fasten it to the headcollar ring at the back of the pony's chin. Turn him out as normal and when you go to catch him take a leadrope and a shallow container with some of his favourite feed or titbits, such as sliced carrots, in it. A washing up bowl is ideal – an ordinary bucket is too deep as the next step will show.

If you turn your pony out in a headcollar, always use a leather one or one which (like this) has breakable rings. Fasten a loop of twine to it if the pony is difficult to catch

Take some feed or titbits in a shallow bucket. When the pony starts to eat, quietly clip the rope on to the loop

If he turns away when he sees you, leave him. Never chase after him; it takes patience but, eventually, he will want to investigate what you have to offer. Keep going into the field with your bowl of titbits and leadrope and when he comes up to you and starts eating, quietly clip the leadrope on to the headcollar loop.

This method means that you do not have to raise your hand and take hold of the headcollar, which many ponies take as the signal to fling up their heads and gallop off. Let him continue eating and make a fuss of him, lead him forwards for a few steps and make a fuss of him again – and then let him go. Unclip the leadrope as quietly as you fastened it, step back and walk off.

Do this a couple more times during the day, then finally catch the pony and take him in to his stable or wherever he is fed at the usual time. Give him his meal and perhaps spend some time grooming him, then either turn him out again or settle him for the night, depending on whether he usually stays in or not.

If you get to bringing-in time and the pony still refuses to be caught, leave him out – all night if necessary – without a feed. He has to realise that he only gets fed if he co-operates. Be patient and follow the method described above for a few times before you ride him. When you decide to ride, let him have a *very small* feed or some titbits first. He will start to associate being caught with a pleasant experience and catching him should be easier.

Ignore people who tell you to 'walk him down' by following him round the field as he walks away from you, or, even worse, those who advise you to round him up into a corner to catch him. A pony's defence from something he does not like is to run away and he is likely to charge for a gap between two people, however small it is.

Nor should you consider tethering a pony, as there have been cases of tethered animals being badly injured or even strangling themselves. It is actually an offence to 'cruelly tether' a horse or pony and anyone who does so could be prosecuted.

Some ponies always demand a little guile from their owners, while others are only difficult to catch at certain times, such as when the first flush of spring grass comes through and is infinitely more appealing than work.

Chewing

Chewing can be an expensive habit and – depending on the pony's choice of what to try his teeth on – may not do his health much good, either. A pony who persistently chews wood can end up with splinters in his stomach or colic or both.

Having said that, chewing is a habit that most youngsters go through while they are teething. Not surprisingly, their mouths are sore at this time and chewing probably helps to relieve the irritation. It cannot go unchecked, though, as it can soon run up expensive damage to stables and equipment.

Some ponies will chew anything that is left in their reach, from reins when they are left tacked up to rugs lying over the stable door. Get into the habit of moving everything possible out of reach and, if you have to leave him tied up with his tack on, twist the reins and thread the throatlatch through them.

As the way to a pony's mind is often through its stomach, convince him that chewing anything but his food leaves a nasty taste in the mouth. There are liquid preparations which can be painted on tack and rugs. These are similar to anti-nail-biting preparations for humans and if you have ever tasted the latter you will know how effective they can be. The best makes are supposed not to damage leather or fabric but it makes sense to use them on old rugs and tack during the 'training period'.

If this does not work on rug chewers, use an anti-chew bib which fastens to the headcollar. You can either buy one from your local saddler or make your own by cutting up a plastic bucket or tub. If you go for the DIY version, make sure there are no sharp edges or splits.

Stable destroyers should be deterred by painting a creosote-type product on the woodwork. The clear variety is less messy to work with and does not stain clothes so badly. You can also buy metal strips from stable joinery specialists to fasten down tempting edges such as those above and down the side of the door.

It is important to work out why the habit has started. In ponies up to five years old, teething is an obvious answer, but boredom and/or a vitamin or mineral deficiency can also be the culprits. Chewing the bark off trees is often a sign of a dietary deficiency, unless the turnout area is so bare that there is nothing else to eat. If older ponies suddenly start chewing, look to these possible reasons first.

Make sure the horse has a mineralised salt lick available. Most take to these readily but a few never seem to get the hang of them. Also add a teaspoon of salt to each feed and make sure the diet is adequate in vitamins and minerals.

This can be difficult with ponies. Even if you feed a mix or nut which is formulated to contain everything they need, many ponies are such good doers that the risk of them getting too fat or contracting laminitis means you cannot feed according to the feed companies' often generous recommendations. In this case, feed the quantities that you have worked out as appropriate for your pony's bodyweight, age, temperament and workload and add a broad-spectrum vitamin and mineral supplement at half the manufacturer's recommended dose.

Clipping

Clipping difficulties are often caused by careless handling or faulty equipment. It is not a problem to try to tackle on your own – clipping should always be done by an experienced adult, especially if you anticipate problems.

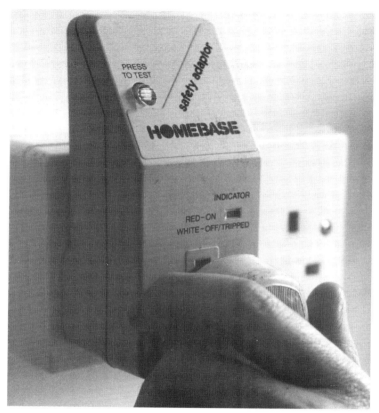

Always use a circuit breaker with electric clippers

Before you start clipping any pony, even if you are sure he will behave perfectly, make sure that you have a clean, dry area to work in and that you have plenty of rugs to hand so that he will not get cold as the clipping progresses. Check that the clipper blades are sharp, at the correct tension and properly oiled. Dull or badly adjusted and maintained blades may get hot and/or pull the hair instead of clipping cleanly; this will be uncomfortable for the pony and, not surprisingly, he will make his objections felt.

If you are using electric clippers, always use a circuit breaker (and always check it before you start). These are cheap to buy but can save lives. If the pony damages the cable, the current will cut out instead of you both being electrocuted. Be careful about the way the cable falls – it is easy to startle a horse into kicking out by letting a cable accidentally touch his back legs.

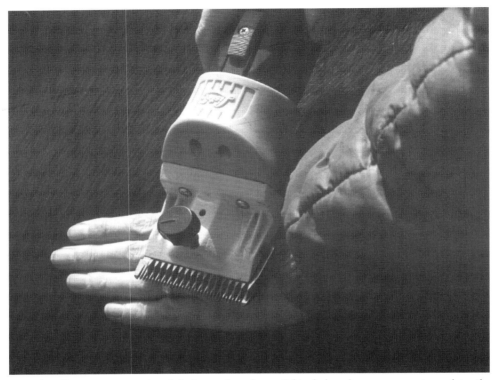

Lay the clippers on your hand before using them. This helps the pony to get used to the vibration

With a pony who is being clipped for the first time, you need a reliable helper to give him confidence. Never start clipping without warning, even when you are dealing with an experienced pony. Let the clippers run for half a minute so that he can get used to the noise: this is especially important with an inexperienced or nervous animal.

If the main problem seems to be noise, you may find that the pony is less upset by quieter, battery-powered clippers (not all battery ones are up to removing thick coats, so do some research before buying a new set). When he seems reasonably happy about the sound of the clippers, lay your hand on his shoulder and rest the clippers on top of your hand. This lessens the amount of vibration and makes for a gentle introduction. He should soon stand calmly and you can then rest the clippers on his shoulder. Gradually, step by step, you should be able to start clipping.

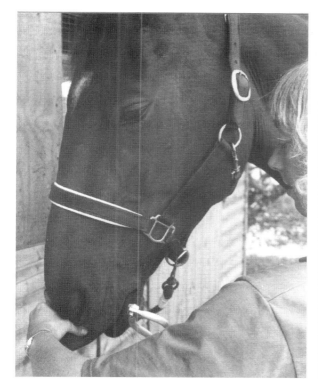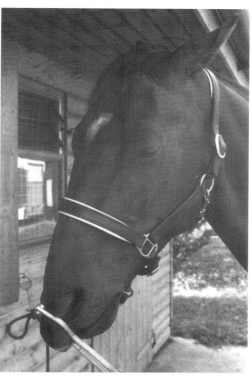

It is better to use a twitch than risk getting hurt. This humane twitch is being applied to the top lip . . . and the wearer soon relaxes!

The best places to start are the shoulders and neck area, as most ponies will accept the clippers here without too much fuss. The 'danger zones' tend to be the head and lower leg areas and some horses are also ticklish on parts of their stomachs.

Start by clipping the parts you can do without fuss, leaving the difficult bits until last. Make sure the pony is kept warm with rugs, as he will fidget if he gets cold. When you get to the difficult parts, or if the pony is difficult despite your patience and careful preparation, use a twitch.

Some people may tell you that twitches are cruel but as long as they are properly adjusted this is not so. The old grooms used to make their own twitches from a loop of string fastened to a short length of broom handle, but now you can buy 'humane twitches' which look like a pair of large metal nutcrackers. The twitch is fitted on the pony's top lip and the pressure created stimulates the production of natural substances called endorphins. These make the pony feel relaxed. In fact, some will actually go to sleep when you twitch them.

Be careful where you stand while you are clipping. Position yourself at the side, because ponies will strike out forwards and backwards but not out to the side. The person clipping and the person holding or twitching the horse must always stand on the same side because a pony will move away from danger, not towards it.

You will need a helper to deal with a pony who does not like having his legs clipped: in fact, in an ideal world you will have two helpers — one to twitch the pony and the other to hold one of his legs up. If you are clipping a front leg your helper will hold up the other front one; if you are clipping a back one, your helper will hold up the *foreleg* on the same side. In other words, if you are clipping the offside hind leg, your helper will need to hold up the offside foreleg.

Another useful technique with ponies who do not like having their hind legs clipped is to put a lot of pressure on the point of the hock, which will block the force of an attempted kick.

If the pony has a ticklish stomach, you will again need someone to hold up one of his legs to prevent him from cow-kicking. It can be a wise precaution to wear a hard hat or skull cap while clipping this kind of customer.

If you are able to clip most of him but he will not stand to have his legs or head clipped, try leaving the legs on in a hunter clip and leave a bridle line on the head. If it is his first time, try giving him a trace clip this time. He may be less worried when you come to clip him again.

Occasionally, you may meet a pony for whom nothing works. You then have two options — you can either give up the idea of clipping and start rugging him in late summer to discourage a thick growth of winter coat, or you can call your vet out to give him a sedative. This will involve the expense of a call-out fee and the drugs but should make the pony dopey enough to be clipped in safety by an experienced operator.

Crib Biting

Crib biting is one of the most annoying vices, especially when it is combined with wind sucking (see separate section). Like all vices, it is much more common in horses than ponies, probably because ponies are nearly always kept out much more of the time and are able to follow a much more natural way of life than stabled horses.

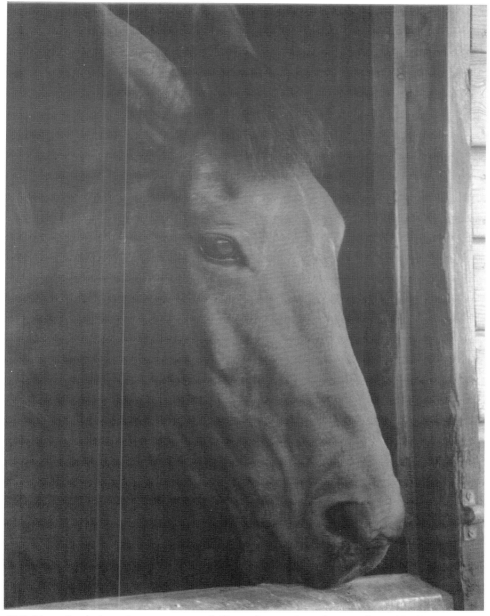

Crib biters fix their teeth on to any available surface, such as the top of a stable door

Crib biters get hold of a handy surface, such as a door ledge or fence post, and bear down on it with their teeth. You can often detect a horse with this vice from the distinctive way the top teeth are worn down. Apart from the fact that it is annoying and antisocial, it can cause a lot of damage – crib biters weaken fences and play havoc with wooden stables.

If you know that a pony is a crib biter (and the seller should disclose this to you), think twice about buying it unless it is perfect for your needs in all other respects. Even then, think carefully: a horse with a vice is more difficult to sell than one without, and if you need to keep him at livery you may find some yard owners reluctant to take him. Many people believe that horses copy others with vices. This is debatable, but few people would want the risk of having their horse stabled next to a crib biter or wind sucker.

However, if the pony is so talented that you are prepared to take the attitude that what he does in his spare time is up to him, there are various measures you can try. The latest research shows that stable vices are a reaction to stress and/or boredom, so make sure the pony has plenty to keep his attention. If his waistline is not a problem, give him hay. To make him eat it more slowly, put it in a net with a small mesh or put one net inside another to achieve the same effect. Leave a radio on outside his stable, tuned to a 'talk' station rather than a music one as some ponies are happier when they can hear voices.

In bad cases, you may have to resort to a cribbing collar, a leather collar with a hinged metal section which fits under the horse's throat. This makes it uncomfortable for the horse when he arches his neck to bite down. Get an expert to check that you have fastened it tightly enough to be effective but not so tight that it causes damage or discomfort. It should be worn with a leather headcollar and a strap going from the headpiece to the cribbing collar to keep it in position, and will need to be removed at feed times.

If the pony always cribs on the same place, such as the top of his stable door, it is possible to fit a short length of electric fencing across here so that when he tries to indulge he will get a very unpleasant but harmless electric shock. Unfortunately, some horses may take this so much to heart that they then refuse to come to the stable door which may, in turn, make them more 'wound up' than ever – you have to assess your particular animal and weigh up the pros and cons before trying this method.

Finally, there is an expensive and traumatic operation called the Forsales operation. This involves sending the horse to a veterinary hospital or centre where an incision is made down the neck and the upper part of the chest and a layer of muscle is shaved off. The idea of this operation is that is removes the horse's ability to arch its neck down to crib but does not prevent him from eating properly or working on the bit and only an expert could tell that it had been performed. It demands a long period of aftercare which may not be possible for some people and although it works in many cases, it cannot be guaranteed.

Escaping from the Field

Ponies are herd animals and like to be part of a group; normally one will only try to escape from his field if he is on his own and wants to get back to his friends. Some are happy to be left on their own while a companion is away for an hour or two, perhaps being ridden, but others will be so worried about being alone that you will have to make sure they cannot hurt themselves.

Some ponies are accomplished escape artists

The ideal situation is one where there are always at least two horses or ponies in the field. If this is impossible, try to find a way of providing companionship for the one who is left behind. Ponies will make friends with donkeys, goats, sheep and even chickens! Another option is to stable the pony who is left behind while his companion works, but only do this if there are other horses on the yard at the time. Shutting a lonely pony in a stable with no others in sight can be a recipe for getting a hole kicked in your stable wall!

Having said that, there are some escape artists who seem to think that the grass is always greener on the other side of the fence and who take great delight in pushing their way through. The first step in thwarting them is obviously to make sure that your fencing is as safe and secure as possible. Thick hedging, combined, if necessary, with post and rail, is the perfect choice but is a rarity these days. Many farmers and livery yards will not use post and rail because it is too costly or because they also want to graze sheep.

If you rent grazing, you usually have to take the best you can get and put up with what is less than perfect. The answer from both a safety and a security point of view is to put up electric fencing, which is quite cheap to buy and easy to put up yourself. There are two types of electric fencing, one designed to be used as a permanent barrier, perhaps on its own, and the other as a temporary set-up or in conjunction with existing fencing. Both can be set up with a 'tape gate' to allow you to get in and out of the field.

Some people will tell you that you should introduce a pony to electric fencing by leading him up to it and touching his nose on it, but this can also be a good way of getting jumped on. It is important that someone stays with him until he has got used to it, but ponies are so curious that this will not usually take long – they are always quick to investigate something new in the field.

Electric fencing gives an unpleasant but harmless shock, as you will find if you touch it yourself. Some ponies only have to touch it once to learn the lesson, while others get two or three shocks before they associate the bite of the electric current with the fencing. Once they have made the association, they will give it a wide berth, so make sure they have a wide entrance and exit to the field when you switch off the current and unhook the tape gates.

Feeding (Aggressive when Feeding)

Ponies that are aggressive when you give them their food can be dangerous if they trap you in the stable. The first step is therefore one of self-preservation

– make sure that you have a clear exit. If you use a manger, make sure it is at the front of the stable rather than at the back so that you do not have to dodge flying hooves on the way out. If the horse will eat from it, you can also use a manger which hooks on to the stable door so that you do not have to go in at all.

Keep a headcollar on the pony at feed times and make sure that you are wearing a thick jacket with long sleeves that will offer protection if he tries to bite you. Carry a short stick as you approach and, if he goes for you, get hold of the headcollar, saying 'No!' in a sharp voice and hit him. You need to take a similar approach as that suggested for the pony that barges – he must learn to step back and wait, rather than dive at you with teeth bared and heels flying. Two pairs of hands are more effective than one; for safety's sake, get a reasonably agile adult to help you.

Feeding (Reluctant to Eat)

The old saying 'eats like a horse' applies to most of them, especially ponies. However, now and then you come across one who is reluctant to eat or who is particularly fussy about what he will or will not welcome in his feed bucket.

Ponies tend to be greedy, but you might find the occasional fussy eater

If the reluctant feeder is a new purchase, do not worry about it too much. Many horses and ponies are wary until they get used to their new home and will not eat properly until they settle down. Just make sure he has plenty of hay and water and offer him small feeds (preferably the same food that his previous owners gave him) with sliced carrots or apples to tempt him.

If this situation persists beyond about a week, however, or a previously healthy appetite fails, you should suspect that something is wrong. The most obvious reason is that the pony has a problem with his teeth; up to the age of five, horses are changing baby teeth for adult ones and can go through a lot of discomfort. Sometimes the milk tooth 'cap', which the adult tooth dislodges, is reluctant to come off, which makes it difficult for the horse to eat. Mature horses need their teeth checking at least once a year and any sharp edges should be rasped.

There are several signs which point to dental problems being the cause. The pony may cross his jaw, drop food back out of his mouth while trying to eat or roll the food into balls in his mouth and drop them on the floor (known as quidding). Get your vet or horse dentist out to check the animal's mouth and carry out any remedial work, such as rasping.

If the pony shows signs of ill health, lack of appetite may be part of it. Watch out for listlessness, sweating and/or shivering, a runny nose and/or cough or a rise in temperature – a normal temperature is about 38°C (100.5°F) in a horse and up to 38.6 (101.5°F) in foals.

A few ponies have naturally small appetites but they are very much the exception. Many find coarse mixes more palatable than nuts and will enjoy sliced apples and carrots mixed in with their feed. The best thing for a jaded appetite is spring grass, so turn the pony out as much as possible unless there is a risk of laminitis.

Grooming

Grooming difficulties usually arise because the pony is thin-skinned and sensitive or has been roughly treated, or both. For safety's sake, always tie him up short enough to prevent him from being able to bite you and make sure you position yourself so that he cannot throw his head up and bang you in the face or kick you. The closer you stand to the side of the horse, the less danger there is of getting kicked.

Using harsh grooming brushes on ticklish or sensitive areas will only make things worse. When working on the head or belly, you may have to use your hand to get the worst of the dried mud off and follow that with a soft body brush or a long-bristled 'soft dandy' of the type designed originally for Thoroughbred racehorses.

Necks, shoulders and bodies are usually not quite so sensitive but you may still have to forget the traditional hard-bristle dandy brushes. Instead, tackle dried mud with one of the new type of rubber grooming tools with flexible prongs. Start off very gently and build up the pressure if the animal tolerates it. Most enjoy it, as it acts as a gentle massage.

Time and patience should lead to better behaviour from your pony, but bad manners should not be tolerated no matter how roughly you think he has been groomed in the past. Attempts to bite and kick should be treated with a sharp word of reprimand and, if he persists, a slap on the girth.

Headshy

Headshy ponies are difficult to handle, especially when you are trying to put on a bridle or headcollar. Start by checking the fit of your tack, as browbands which are too tight and pinch the base of the ears are a frequent cause. Then eliminate possible physical causes, with your vet's help if necessary – these include ear mites, teeth problems and sight defects.

If everything checks out as normal, you then have to decide whether the pony has been frightened by previous rough handling or is simply being stroppy. If he is nervous, you will have to spend time gaining his confidence and getting him used to being handled; this is one of the few occasions when giving him titbits can be justified. Talk to him and scratch him between the eyes. Most horses love this and some will go to sleep while you make a fuss of them.

You will gradually be able to build up to stroking his face, scratching under his jaw and round the base of his ears and pulling his ears gently through your hands. Some ponies dislike having their ears touched, often because they have been bridled roughly or ear-twitched in the past.

If he is just being naughty – for instance, if he throws up his head to avoid having the bridle put on and you are sure there is no pain or discomfort, then try the techniques covered in the bitting and bridling section. Use a headcollar and leadrope to form a 'standing martingale' and be quiet, but insistent, until he behaves.

Once you have cured the problem, remember never, ever to hit the pony on the head region, otherwise you will undo all the good work and put yourself back to square one.

Kicking

Any horse or pony will lash out in fright if something startles him – for instance, if a dog rushes up to chase him. However, when kicking becomes a habit, you have a discipline problem that must be sorted out before someone gets hurt.

Make sure that, whenever you handle the pony, you position yourself in the least vulnerable position close to his side. It is sensible to wear a hard hat or skull cap when you are dealing with him; this could save your life if you are unlucky enough to be kicked on the head.

If you have to stand or walk round behind him (and this should obviously be avoided as far as possible), then you must either be so far away from him that he cannot possibly reach you, or so close that he cannot draw his leg up and back to lash out. An experienced handler can usually prevent kicking by pressing hard on the point of the hock, which, again, prevents him from moving into kicking position.

If he tends to kick when he is being clipped, you must take every precaution and have an experienced adult helper (see the section on clipping). Ticklish ponies often cow-kick when they are being groomed, so avoid hard-bristle brushes on sensitive areas.

An isolated kick out that is a reaction to fright can be ignored but kicking that is the pony's way of saying 'leave me alone' must be punished. Use your voice and also hit him immediately he lashes out.

Kicking the Door

Kicking the door at feeding time, or to get attention, might not seem too bad a habit – until you have to put up with it! As well as being noisy and irritating, it can cause soundness problems: the pony who does it repeatedly can soon injure a leg. If it goes on long enough, he can end up with a 'big knee' because of the build-up of fluid caused by repeated blows.

Scold him when he does it but do not expect this to cure the habit. A short, sharp shock, such as squirting water at him from a large plant sprayer, or even throwing a bucket of water at him, sometimes works. Another deterrent for some ponies is to nail prickly coconut matting to the inside of the stable door. This will cushion the blow to his leg and be uncomfortable.

If possible, it can be a good idea to fit door chains or a removable bar across your stable door. (You can even use an ordinary leadrope with a quiet type.) This enables you to leave the door open but prevents the pony from walking out – unless he is the limbo dancing type. It has been known!

Leading

There are two common problems with leading: one is the pony who lags behind and refuses to keep up with you and the other is the one who charges off regardless of the person at the other end of the leadrope. Whatever category yours falls into, use a bridle rather than a headcollar and leadrope to give you more control. Incidentally, if you have to lead on the road you should *always* use a bridle, even with the quietest horse.

If you are dealing with a real thug, it is sensible to use a Chifney or anti-rearing bit rather than your ordinary one – even if he shows no inclination to rear, you will find the extra control it provides invaluable. However, as with all potentially strong bits, it must be used with care.

With the reluctant leader, try to find an area with a wall or solid fence as a teaching ground. Position him so that the wall is on one side of him and you are on the other and stand at his shoulder so that you are in line with his front legs. Carry a schooling whip and click with your tongue when you want him to walk on; if he takes no notice or does not move off sharply, give him a smack.

Be prepared for him jumping forwards and take care not to give him a jab in the mouth. Praise him and keep on repeating the lesson until he associates the click with the smack and walks out smartly when he hears the verbal command alone. You may need to practise this for 20 minutes a day for a while, especially if you want to show him (when you will have to trot him up in hand for the judge).

At first you may need an assistant to click from behind as well but you should dispense with this as soon as possible. Eventually, you will be able to lead him without the support of the wall but at first this prevents him from evading the schooling whip by moving his quarters over and walking like a crab. If he goes back to his old ways, give him a refresher course using the wall.

Once he has learned his lesson, he should walk, and later trot, with an active but not hurried stride. You should be at his shoulder and the reins should be loose enough not to restrict his head carriage. It is important to look forwards: never look back and try to drag him along. You will simply set up a pulling contest which even the smallest pony is bound to win.

A Chifney is essential for the pony who charges off. He should be dealt with by an adult, who stands level with his head and gives a sharp 'pull and release' when he tries to go. It must be a definite take and give; a solid pull will only give the animal something to lean on.

If you have problems when you take your pony to the field, see the section on turning out.

Loading

As long as they are introduced to it quietly and sensibly, most ponies accept travelling in a box or trailer as just another part of life. However, if they are frightened or given a rough ride – either because of poor driving ability or the state of the vehicle – they may, not surprisingly, decide that they do not want anything to do with it. There is also the odd rebel who simply says, 'Not today, thank you!'.

If a previously good traveller suddenly becomes difficult to load, check that none of the above factors is to blame. The important things about driving a horsebox or towing a trailer are smooth acceleration, braking and gear changes, anticipation and observation. For instance, if you see a roundabout ahead, you will need to start slowing down far earlier than in a car – and you also need to watch out for changes in camber.

Your vehicle should be light, airy and inviting. It is asking too much to expect a pony to walk into a black hole, especially if he associates it with a jolting ride to come.

You must also make sure that he has plenty of room to spread his legs and keep his balance. Many people make the mistake of moving partitions closer to the pony in the mistaken idea that this will give him more support, when in fact this is the worst thing you can do. Move the partition over or, if necessary, take it out altogether. Some ponies will only travel happily in a two-horse trailer if they have it all to themselves with no centre partition.

Loading a reluctant or nervous animal takes a mixture of firmness, patience and confidence. If you do not think you can manage, it is worth hiring a professional, licensed transporter for half a day to help you. Choose someone who has a good reputation for the way they handle the horses in their care and explain your problem; most good transporters will be happy to help, although obviously you will have to pay the going rate for their time.

The pony should be protected with the right equipment and he should be used to wearing it. It is often a good idea to put on his travelling gear for a while even when he is not going anywhere. That way, he does not automatically associate travelling boots or bandages with what is to him the trauma of loading. Youngsters should be accustomed to travelling gear before they even see a horsebox or trailer, as it often takes a while for them

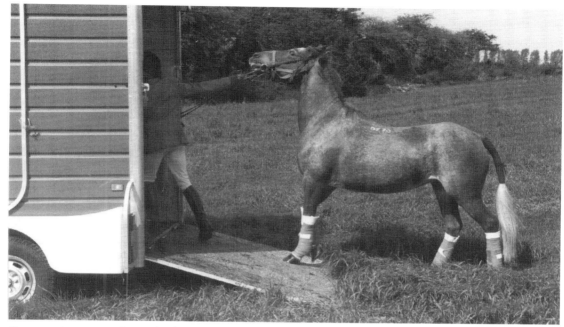

Some ponies are naughty to load even when the vehicle is light and inviting

to get completely used to the feel of leg protection and a tail bandage.

The essentials are a leather headcollar, tail bandage and, if necessary, tailguard and bandages over padding or boots. Never travel a pony in a nylon headcollar. If he panics, a leather one will break before he hurts himself but his neck may snap before a nylon one does.

A pollguard is a good safeguard for a pony who may throw up his head (which usually applies to any animal who does not want to be loaded). You must also use at least a snaffle bridle over the headcollar, but preferably a Chifney (see the section on leading). Take off the noseband and, when the pony is safely loaded, tie him up and remove the bridle. Never leave it on for the journey, as he could damage his mouth if the bit rings got caught up.

Set aside plenty of time when trying to reform a difficult loader and have two experienced adults on hand. Kit out the horse as above and park the horsebox or trailer so that the interior is light and clearly visible. You should have a wall or solid post and rail fence to one side and preferably behind, if possible (making sure there is still enough room to lower the ramp and lead the animal straight up).

Ask two helpers to fix a lunge line to each side of the trailer

There is a range of methods you can use to encourage him to load and it is usually a matter of seeing what works best! Whatever you try, it is important that you keep looking forwards. Looking back at the pony or, even worse, turning round and trying to drag him in, is useless. Make sure the person leading and the helpers are all wearing gloves, boots with steel toecaps and hard hats or skull caps.

Food is a useful incentive for a greedy pony. Put a bucket of food on the ground in front of the ramp, then gradually move it to the edge of the ramp, then up the ramp so that the animal has to put his feet on the ramp to get at it.

Some horses seem to worry about whether a ramp is solid or not, in the same way that inexperienced ones are naturally cautious about going through water when they cannot see the bottom. Picking up a front foot and placing it on the ramp can help; do not worry if the pony paws at the ramp a few times, as he is just testing whether it seems safe or not.

It often helps to fasten a lunge line to each side of the vehicle. A helper should hold each one and stand to the side. As the pony is led forward, the helpers can cross over behind, well out of kicking range. The lunge reins can be used to put pressure on his rear end and encourage him forwards, but they must not be allowed to slip down over his hocks or up over his back.

They should then cross over and apply gentle pressure with the lines to encourage the pony to walk forwards

If only one person is available to help, a similar technique can be tried with a single lunge line. However, this is not usually so effective

Eventually, the pony should load without the aid of the lunge lines, although it is always wise to keep them available

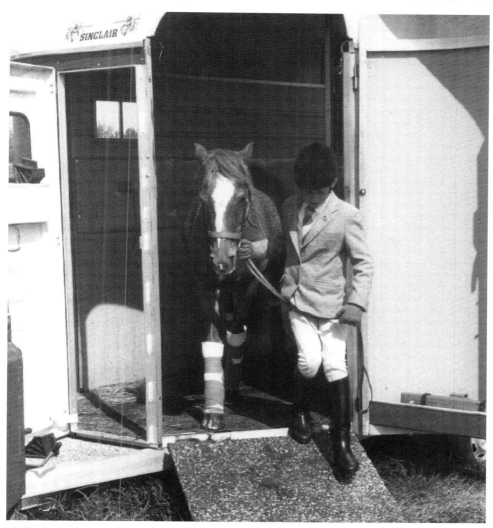

Walk the pony out of the vehicle as calmly and carefully as you walk him in

If the pony is not frightened but is being plain awkward, someone who knows how to give it one good wallop on the quarters with a lunge whip, without tangling the whip round his legs or getting within kicking distance, can be very useful. You do not have to have quite the skills of Indiana Jones, but handling a lunge whip well does take practice.

The pony must face the ramp and the person leading must be prepared for him to shoot forwards when the whip makes contact. Click your tongue to encourage him to keep going and make a fuss of him and reward him with a titbit when he is in the box.

Other forms of encouragement for the definitely naughty pony include pushing a bristle yardbroom against his rear end, throwing small pebbles or water at his quarters or flicking his heels gently with a lunge whip until he moves forwards out of irritation. The last method takes some dexterity if you are to avoid wrapping the lunge whip round the pony's legs, so send for Indiana Jones again or practise on a fence post first.

Loading problems are not solved in a single lesson. You will have to practise every day for some time until the pony accepts loading and unloading as part of his normal routine.

Whatever else you do, when faced with a reluctant loader it is vital that you do not lose your temper or begin to shout. This will only make matters worse.

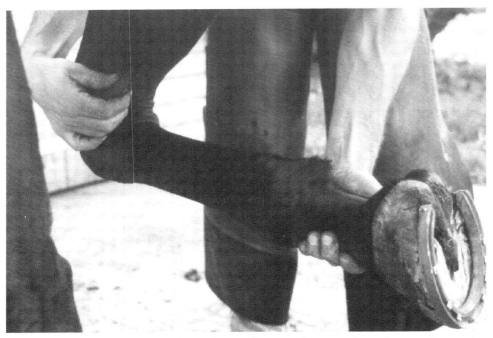

If your pony will not pick up his feet, ask your farrier to show you this technique of squeezing the chestnut

Picking up Feet

All youngsters should be taught to pick up their feet when asked. It takes them some time to get used to the idea of standing on three legs, so, when teaching your foal, make sure he is standing in a balanced position to start with. If his legs are splayed out when you ask him to lift a foot off the ground, you may overbalance him.

If you have an older, awkward animal, get your farrier to show you how to handle him. Farriers are better than anyone else at persuading ponies who do not want to lift their feet that it is a good idea to comply. It is a matter of technique rather than strength. If you have an awkward customer who

Make sure he is standing in a balanced position before trying to pick up his foot

simply leans back when you put pressure on his leg and shoulder, get hold of the chestnut on the leg you want him to lift and squeeze it hard. As he bends his leg in response, take hold of the bottom part quickly.

Most ponies will give in gracefully once they grasp the idea and realise that the only alternative is discomfort. If you always pick up the feet in the same order, e.g. near fore, near hind, off hind, off fore, he will soon anticipate and may even begin to pick up the next foot without you asking.

Pulling Mane and Tail

Before you get too enthusiastic about this, remember that native ponies should be shown in their natural state (although tidying up is accepted) and ponies who live out are best left with full tails to protect the dock from flies.

The best time to pull manes and tails is after exercise, when the pony is warm, as the hair then comes out more easily. Do a little bit at a time over several days and use a good anti–irritant shampoo to soothe the area.

It is always safer to use a twitch than to struggle with an animal who objects. Pulling tails can be particularly dangerous and should only be attempted by experienced adults.

Tie the pony up in a confined space (a stall is ideal) and stack straw bales behind his back legs so that there is at least one bale between you and a kick. The confined space prevents the pony from moving sideways and the straw bales pushed up against his legs mean that he cannot kick you.

If he objects to having his mane and tail pulled to the extent that his behaviour puts the handler in danger, forget the idea of pulling and use a thinning knife instead or thinning scissors. Whatever method you use, you will need to bandage the tail regularly to keep it in shape.

Saddling

Ponies who object to having their saddles put on do so because someone or something has made them uncomfortable or because the saddle is causing pain. Check for obvious causes like back problems and girth galls and make sure that your saddle, rugs and rollers (if used) fit well. This might sound obvious, but a lot of people ride on badly fitting tack. (See the introduction to the riding section for guidelines on fitting saddles and bridles.)

Once these problems have been eliminated, tie the pony up and put the saddle on quietly, sliding it back into position so that the coat hairs lie flat. Whatever sort of numnah you choose, it should be wrinkle-free and pulled

Previous rough handling can make ponies difficult to saddle

up into the front saddle arch so that it does not press down on the withers. It should also be washed regularly in a non-biological detergent – some ponies are allergic to the biological ones and develop skin irritations.

Fasten the girth fairly loosely to start with, just tight enough to keep the saddle in place. Keep your actions smooth: do not jerk on the girth straps to fasten them. Leave the pony tied up securely for ten minutes with his saddle on, or lead him round for a couple of minutes, then tighten the girth gradually. If he is really sensitive, lead him round for a few minutes more before you get on.

Before you mount, check that the girth is tight enough and pull each foreleg forwards in turn so that the skin is smooth underneath and around the girth. Stand the pony facing a wall or fence, or ask a helper to stand at his head, and either get someone to give you a leg-up or use a mounting block. This makes it easier to land lightly in the saddle and avoids the risk of pulling the saddle over, as can happen all too easily when you mount from the ground.

Keep an even rein contact, even if the pony has been known to try to bite you when you get on. If you have one rein too short and he tries to move off, he can become so unbalanced that he will slip or even fall over. A favourite pony trick is to try to bite your boot; this calls for an experienced, lightweight adult who can bring the toe of his or her boot into sharp contact with the pony's nose. They soon decide that it is not such a good idea after all!

Shoeing

The best person to deal with a pony who is difficult to shoe is a good farrier. However, while his experience in handling naughty or nervous animals will be invaluable, you will have to do your bit too.

The section on picking up feet will help you to deal with this kind of resistance. The next step is to tap the pony's feet with a dandy brush, imitating the farrier's actions but not impacting the same shock to the foot as the farrier does when he nails on a shoe. (Shoeing does not cause any pain unless the nails go into the wrong place, but some ponies dislike the vibration of having the nails banged in.)

When he accepts having his feet tapped with the brush, move on to doing the same thing with a hammer. If he is particularly spooky, fitting blinkers may help – but do not try to winch up his leg or tie up one leg while the farrier works on another. This is a surefire recipe for an accident, as the pony may well struggle and then fall over.

If the situation is so bad that even your farrier says the horse is impossible, you will either have to get the vet out to sedate the animal or try glue-on shoes. Both methods are expensive.

Tying Up

The pony who learns that he can break away if he pulls back when tied up is infuriating, but can be cured. No matter how annoying this habit is, you must *always* tie up to a piece of string rather than direct to a tying-up ring. Many animals will panic if they pull back and meet strong resistance. The result could be a pony with a broken neck, a badly damaged stable or both. It is essential that, in a crisis, the string will break, freeing the animal.

The best way to teach a youngster to tie up, or to reform an older animal who does not like it, is to use a wooden ball and rope like those designed for use in stalls. This will restrict him but still allow him to move his head – most horses take to it quite happily. If he starts to move back you can encourage him forwards with your voice. Try to tie him up so that there is a barrier behind him; horses do not like backing into things.

If you cannot rig up a ball and rope system, you can try using a lunge line, although this is not as satisfactory. Clip the lunge line to the horse's headcollar and pass it through a tying-up ring and back to your hand. When the pony pulls back, you have to play him like a fish, giving and taking until he realises either that there is nothing to be frightened of or that he is wasting his time.

When you tie a pony up, give him enough leeway to move his head. Tying up too short is a common cause of horses breaking away.

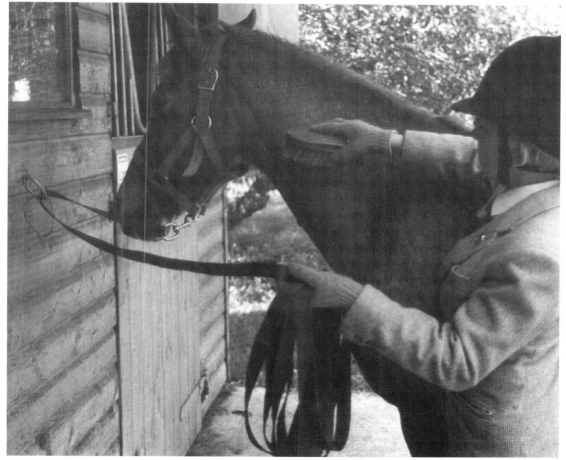

Teach a pony to accept being tied up by using a lunge line passed through the tying-up ring. This enables you to 'give and take'

Turning Out

Some ponies are so eager to get out to the field that they try to drag you there. Even worse are the ones who try to throw up their heads and gallop off as soon as they are through the gate, regardless of whether or not you are at the other end of the leadrope.

The first step is to follow the guidelines in the section on leading and use a bridle with a bit over your headcollar. The handler, who should be a confident adult, should turn the pony to face the gate and make him stand for a moment while they remove the bridle and headcollar. Give him a titbit if he behaves and then step back quietly. If he tries to pull away, give a short, sharp tug on the rein and use your voice to reprimand him.

No matter how quiet the pony, always make him face the gate when you let him go and always do it quietly. Just step back and walk quietly away – never slap him on the quarters and encourage him to gallop off or you might set up a bad habit.

Some ponies are very enthusiastic when being turned out

Weaving

The same advice applies to weaving as to the other main stable vices (see box walking, crib biting and wind sucking) – unless the pony is perfect in every other respect or the price reflects the vice, think twice about buying the pony. Vices make a horse harder to sell and may make you unpopular in livery yards.

Weaving varies in degree. At one end of the scale you have the horse who moves his head from side to side and may only do this when he knows he is about to be fed. At the other, you have an animal who rocks his whole body, shifting his weight and stamping down on one leg and then the other. He is the worst prospect, because he is putting wear and tear on his limbs.

Horses do not crib bite, weave, wind suck or box walk in the wild – these are all behaviour patterns that *we* have brought on by the artificial way in

A grid like this may discourage weaving. Standing a weaver in a stall, with companions on either side, is an even better deterrent

which we keep them. The best way to cope with a weaver is to turn him out as much as possible and, when he needs to be in, keep him in a stall with other horses on either side. Removing the top kicking boards between two stables, so that the occupants can see each other and touch noses, also works in some cases, as long as the ponies like each other and do not decide to kick the rest of the wall down.

This is not always possible for the person who has to keep a pony at livery. In this case, keep the pony out as much as possible and fit a V-shaped, anti-weaving grid to his stable door. This still enables him to look out and discourages all but the most determined weaver.

You can also put up a full grid, but this will effectively turn your stable into a prison and usually causes more problems than it cures. It might deter the horse from weaving at first, but he may start weaving behind the door.

A weaver needs to be kept occupied, so make sure that he always has hay while he is stabled. Some horses like to play with 'toys', such as old footballs or indestructible stable buckets (without handles) or skips.

Stable vices are common on racing yards, mainly because racehorses are kept stabled for 22 or 23 hours out of 24. Some trainers recommend letting the horse share his stable with a small companion, such as a sheep or a goat: again, this might not be too popular with a livery yard!

Wind Sucking

Wind sucking is a vice that is very closely related to crib biting, although not all crib biters will wind suck. The horse gulps in lungfuls of air, often latching its teeth on to a surface such as a stable door top at the same time – although some can do it anywhere, even while standing out in the field.

If you are thinking of buying a pony with this vice, think again. It can cause all sorts of digestive upsets, including colic, and the horse will often look pot-bellied because his belly becomes distended with the air he has swallowed.

Wind sucking is often incurable. If the horse crib bites as well, you can try fitting a cribbing collar (see the crib biting section) and hope that he does not learn to do it in isolation. If he only wind sucks in his stable, keep him out as much as possible – although most offenders can also learn to do it by getting hold of fence posts.

Anti-wind sucking bits are available, designed to be worn in the stable, but these are not often successful. They have hollow mouthpieces with holes drilled over the surface and are supposed to prevent the horse from being able to gulp down air.

Riding and Schooling

It is all too easy to plunge into the depths of despair when you watch a beautifully schooled pony going like a dream and then compare it with your own uncooperative/resistant/reluctant animal. However, before you decide to give up riding altogether and switch to something better be-haved, such as a bicycle, remember that there is no such thing as the perfect pony. Everyone has schooling problems at some time or other, because when you ride you have two independent personalities trying to communicate with each other and it is inevitable that the wires will become crossed occasionally.

There can be all sorts of reasons for problems, ranging from lack of understanding (from you, the pony, or both!) to discomfort from sharp teeth or badly fitting tack. You also have to remember that even though you may be pressing all the theoretically correct buttons, you will not get the right response unless the pony has been trained to understand what the aids mean. You cannot simply read a book like this, work out how to ask for a turn on the forehand or half-pass and expect the pony to comply. If he could read too, life would be much simpler!

Whatever the problem, start by checking that the pony is comfortable. Your vet or horse dentist will check that his mouth and teeth are in good condition and your vet will also look at any other possible physical causes. For instance, if a pony shies a lot it is worth getting his eyesight and hearing checked, if only to rule out the obvious.

Does your tack fit the pony and is it adjusted correctly? If you have the slightest doubt, get expert advice. If your saddle pinches the pony, you cannot really blame him for bucking, and if his bit is the wrong size or his browband pinches his ears, it is not surprising if he resists and throws his head about. All of this may sound obvious but when you are trying to find a way round a problem it is often the obvious that gets overlooked (and leaves you feeling like an idiot when someone else points it out).

A bit that is too small will pinch the pony's mouth, while one that is too big will slide from side to side, also causing discomfort. A bit that is too large will also hang too low in the pony's mouth and this will encourage him to put his tongue over it.

There should be a gap the width of an adult's little finger between the bit rings and the pony's mouth on each side. A snaffle bit should wrinkle the corners of the lips and a pelham or Kimblewick should fit snugly into them.

If you use a drop, Flash or Grakle noseband, it should be adjusted to prevent the pony from opening his mouth too far, but not fastened so tightly that he cannot flex his jaw. If it is too tight, he will fight it and find other evasions.

A broad cavesson noseband, fastened tighter than normal and dropped down a hole below the ordinary fitting, is often just as effective. This or a 'doubleback' cavesson, which can be fastened snugly without pinching, can be very effective with curb action bits such as pelhams and Kimblewicks. When adjusting your cavesson you must make sure that you do not interfere with the pony's breathing.

Saddles should be fitted by experts: ask your instructor to recommend a good saddler. Not all saddles are well designed; many have panels that are too narrow and create pressure points, a common cause of sore backs. When you are sitting on the pony you should have clearance at all times between the pommel and his wither and there should be a clear channel of daylight along the pony's spine. Your saddler will also need to check that the saddle does not pinch his shoulders when he moves and that the gullet gives sufficient clearance on either side of the spine.

The other thing to remember about tack is that you might have to change some of it, at least temporarily. It is all very well saying that a pony should be ridden in a snaffle, but if this means that he is in charge of where you are going and at what speed, theory has to give way to safety.

Sometimes it is better to use a bit with a different action, such as a pelham, to give you control. Too many people fall into the trap of believing that a snaffle is always the kindest bit; if you have to try to remove the pony's teeth with it in order to stop him, it definitely is not. A pelham in gentle hands is far kinder than a snaffle in rough ones.

By all means aim to ride in a snaffle and cavesson noseband as long as you feel safe. However, if the pony has learned to open his mouth, lean on the bit and tank off with you at 90 miles an hour, be realistic. Change his bit or noseband for one that makes him listen to you rather than ignoring you, and carry on with your schooling until you get the desired response.

Is the pony being naughty because he is getting too much to eat and is simply 'over the top'? Far too many ponies, especially native ones, are overfed. This is not helped by the fact that too many feed manufacturers' guidelines are over-generous.

Most ponies can be worked totally off grass during spring and summer (and may well even need their grazing restricted because of the risk of laminitis). The pony who works hard during autumn and winter may need small concentrate feeds in addition to hay but do ask an expert before stuffing him with concentrates and do not be tempted to feed high-powered supplements intended for competition horses.

In the past couple of years, herbal specialists and feed companies have developed herbal mixes said to have a relaxing effect on nervous or stressed animals. These do not have a sedative effect and can be successful in some, but not all, cases. It is very important not to exceed the manufacturers' feeding guides.

It is very difficult – in fact, sometimes impossible – to solve schooling problems on your own. You need an 'eye on the ground', someone experienced enough to be able to see if you are giving the right signals and to suggest ways of making them clearer.

All riders, no matter how experienced, make mistakes or get into bad habits. That is why even Olympic stars have trainers or people they go to every now and again for advice and constructive criticism. It is very easy to think that you are doing something properly when you are not (or, just as awkward, to do something wrong without realising).

For instance, you might not realise that you are sitting lopsided or using too much hand and not enough leg. Yet both can put your pony off balance and make it difficult for him to go nicely, even when he is willing to try. Put yourself in balance and the pony will do the same.

The obvious person to go to for help is a good instructor and one of the best ways to find one is through your local Pony Club or riding club. As well as getting good instruction, the cost of which is usually subsidised through the club, you will meet other people with ponies. Solving a problem is much easier when there are other people around to boost your morale.

Ideally, you should have a lesson once a week. Anything is better than nothing, though, so if you can only manage once a month, make the most of it. Your teacher will set you off on the right road and give you things to work on until the next lesson – and if you can persuade a reasonably knowledge-able friend or relative to watch the lesson, he or she can help your schooling at home by reminding you what the instructor said.

Few of us are lucky enough to have manèges or indoor schools, which makes it very annoying when you pick up a book or watch a video which assumes that you have excellent facilities at your disposal. If you can find a level, enclosed area to work in, you have a headstart: if not, you have to improvise and find a way round it.

A corner of a field can make a perfectly adequate schooling area. Marking out a 'dressage arena' with cones or large plastic bottles weighed down with sand or water will give you reference points for riding circles and transitions.

When the ground is too wet to ride on, you can still school out on your hacks. Provided you are on a quiet road, you can practise transitions in walk, trot and halt (*not* canter) between one telegraph pole and the next. If you have quiet tracks or bridleways to ride on, leg yield from one side to the other when you can see that it is safe to do so.

Schooling in the open means that you have to keep your wits about you. Riding a perfect turn on the forehand is one thing; riding it and coming face to face with a tractor you had not noticed coming up behind you is quite another. This kind of schooling makes you and your pony think, which can offer another advantage – when you get to a competition, your pony will probably behave better than the ones who are only used to working in schools and cannot cope with any distractions.

So how do you define schooling? If the very mention of the word conjures up visions of trotting round in circles until you and the pony are dizzy and/or fed up, there is no wonder neither of you enjoys it.

Schooling is simply teaching your pony to understand your aids so that he is comfortable, obedient and enjoyable to ride. It means that he carries himself in balance so that he feels responsive and ready to carry out your next instruction and is ready to stop, start and change gait or direction as soon as you ask him to.

Getting to this stage takes time, especially with a young or badly trained pony, but there is nothing mysterious or complicated about it. As long as you have a reasonably secure seat, understand what you are asking the pony to do and have someone experienced to help you, you can and will improve the way he goes.

Watch a pony trotting and cantering round his field and you will see that he has no trouble turning and keeping his balance, often at great speed. Put a rider on that same pony and he may look uncoordinated and ungainly. The

You can school your pony anywhere where the ground is flat and the going is good

reason for this is that by making him carry a rider's weight, we affect his centre of gravity and throw him off balance – he has to learn to rebalance himself, bring his hind legs further underneath him and take his weight off his forehand.

A well-schooled pony can still behave badly in that he can nap, buck, rear or whatever, but it is always worth persevering with your schooling because you can turn it to your advantage in a crisis. For instance, once the pony understands leg yielding (moving forwards and sideways away from your leg aids), you can use this to help to prevent him from spooking and shying.

The best place to start teaching a pony to move away from the leg is actually in the stable. Hold his headcollar and use your hand on the girth to nudge him over. Use your voice at the same time: say 'Over' as you give the aid.

Try the same thing outside, then while you are riding – if necessary, ask a helper on the ground to reinforce your leg aid by pushing him over as you did in the stable. This is the start of turn on the forehand, where the pony's hindlegs cross over and travel in a small circle round the inside foreleg.

Leg yielding continues this lesson. The easiest way to teach it is down the long side of an arena or alongside your field fence. Start off about 10 m (11 yd) out from the fence and ride straight. If you are on the left rein, you will leg yield to the right. Ask for a slight bend with the left rein, put the left leg slightly behind the girth and nudge the pony forwards and sideways back to the fence, supporting him and controlling his speed with your right hand and leg.

To leg yield to the left, ask for right bend and use your right leg to move him over to the left, supporting with the left hand and leg. At first it may seem a bit like trying to pat your head and rub your stomach at the same time, but start in walk and be pleased with a little at a time. The most important thing is to keep the pony going *forwards* as well as sideways.

Throughout this section you will find that transitions and half-halts are suggested as part of your schooling. Transitions are the posh name for moving up and down from one gait to another – halt to walk, walk to trot and so on. Half-halts build on this: as the name suggests, it is not quite a halt, rather more of a hesitation than a complete stop.

In its simplest form, a half-halt will be a trot transition back down to two or three paces of walk and then a move up to trot again. At the other end of the scale, it is a barely perceptible rebalancing of the horse.

Think of a half-halt as riding up to a closed door that opens just as you reach it. Ride forwards, close your fingers on the reins and sit up extra straight as if you were coming to a halt, then, as the pony starts to obey, open your fingers and close your legs to push him on again.

A famous dressage trainer (that dreaded word again) once said that the half-halt is the aspirin of riding – use one as soon as anything goes wrong! It helps the pony to put himself in balance, which is a major step towards curing a lot of schooling problems.

Improvements usually come gradually. You have to accept that ponies, like people, have different temperaments. Any pony can be schooled so that he becomes a nicer ride but you will never turn a livewire into a plod or vice versa.

If you feel that your and your pony's temperaments are too different for you to form a partnership, find him a home with someone who will enjoy him more than you do and then find yourself a more compatible replacement. You will both be much happier in the long run.

Bitting Problems

Resisting the bit is a common problem. All ponies resist at some time or another, either because they find it difficult to do what you have asked or because they simply do not want to. When the resistance becomes a habit, however, you need to take a closer look.

Once you have asked your vet or horse dentist to check that your pony's mouth and teeth are in good shape and you are sure that your riding is not to blame, look at the shape of his mouth to see if the bit you are using takes this into account. Just as ponies have different-shaped bodies, they also have different-shaped mouths. Some have short mouths, some have longer ones, some have fleshier lips and tongues than others and so on.

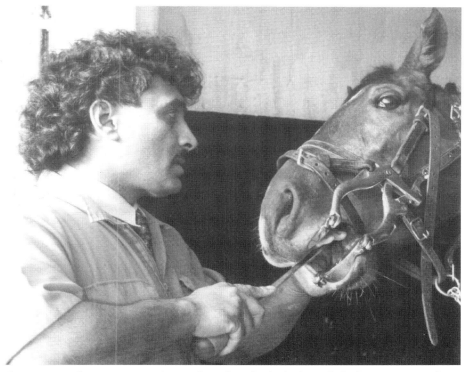

It is important to have your pony's mouth and teeth checked regularly by your vet or horse dentist. Here, Gary Singh Khakhian, a horse dentist whose work takes him all over the world, is rasping the sharp edges on this animal's teeth. The special gag does not hurt the horse, but holds his mouth open so that the dentist or vet can work in safety

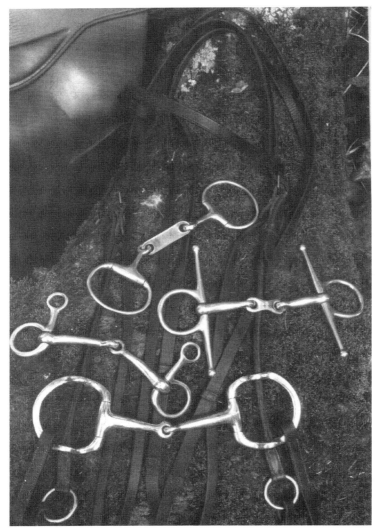

These bits all belong to the snaffle family, but have different actions. From the top, clockwise: Dr Bristol; full-cheek, French link snaffle; gag snaffle with two reins; hanging snaffle.

The flat plate of the Dr Bristol puts pressure on the tongue and some ponies respect it. Do not confuse it with the French link, which has a kidney-shaped link and is often preferred by ponies with fat tongues. The gag snaffle acts as an ordinary snaffle when the top rein is used, but is much stronger when the bottom one is applied. The hanging snaffle applies some poll pressure to help to persuade the pony to lower his head

Two sorts of pelham. The top one has a mild nylon mouthpiece and an elastic curb chain; it is used here with two reins. The bottom one has a metal mouthpiece and curb chain and is fitted with roundings to allow the use of a single rein

On rare occasions, you even get ponies whose teeth grow in the 'wrong' places so that there is literally no room for a bit. You would think that this would be so obvious that it would be noticed pretty quickly but one of the authors knows of a mare who went through five homes in as many months and was condemned as unridable before a horse dentist pointed out that there was not enough space for a bit to rest on the bars of her mouth. When ridden in a bitless bridle, she went beautifully.

A lot of people will tell you that a thick bit is always the kindest sort but this is not necessarily true. Apart from the fact that any bit is only as kind (or severe) as the hands at the other end of the reins, if the pony has a large, fleshy tongue he will find a thick bit uncomfortable.

If this sounds like your pony, try him in either a French link snaffle, which has a kidney-shaped central joint, or a thin snaffle – perhaps even the bridoon from a double bridle. If you want to ride him in a Kimblewick or

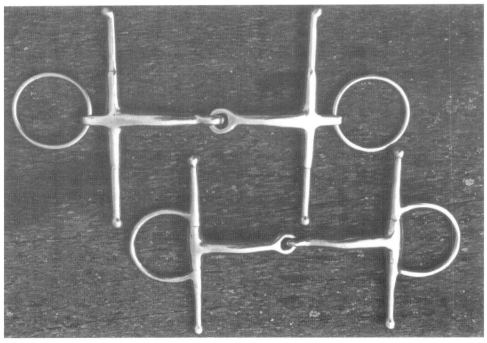

Two kinds of cheek snaffle, which may help if you have steering problems. The Fulmer snaffle at the top has loose rings, which allow a little more play on the mouthpiece than the full-cheek, eggbutt-sided cheek snaffle below

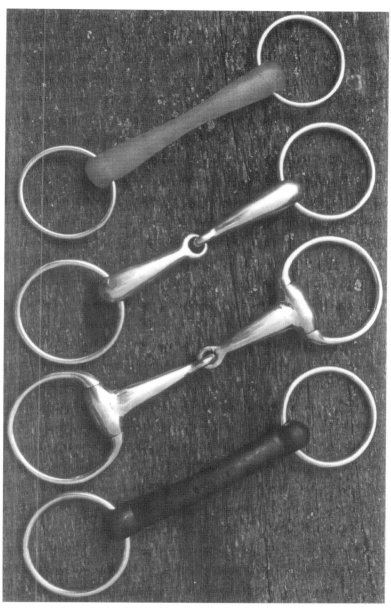

These snaffles are all mild bits, in the right hands – a plastic Nathe snaffle; a hollow-mouth, loose ring; a hollow-mouth eggbutt and a loose ring, mullen-mouth vulcanite

pelham, choose one which has a small port to allow room for the tongue.

Ponies with short mouths and thick necks often go better in mullen-mouthed (half-moon-shaped) bits than jointed ones. Try a loose ring vulcanite snaffle if the pony is an easy ride, but if he uses the strength of his neck to pull, go for a vulcanite pelham. If you can manage them, two reins give a more definite action than one rein and pelham roundings.

When you are choosing a snaffle, the type of cheekpiece you use has a marked effect on the bit's action. A loose ring bit allows more play and is better for the pony who comes above the bit, as he cannot set himself against it. A fixed cheekpiece, such as an eggbutt, moves less in the mouth and encourages the pony who drops behind the bit to take a contact.

If your pony is so frightened of the bit that he throws his head in the air as soon as you pick up the reins, perhaps because he has been ridden by someone with rough hands, it can often help to ride him in two pairs of reins. Use a drop noseband and attach one pair of reins to the noseband rings and the other pair to the bit rings.

Hold the reins as you would those of a pelham or double bridle, with the noseband reins on the outside to start off with so that they are the 'dominant' ones. Progress gradually from riding solely on the noseband reins to riding on the noseband reins and also taking a very light contact on the bit reins. With time and patience, you should be able to discard the noseband reins and ride on the bit ones.

Alternatively, you could try a bitless bridle. If you want to compete in anything other than endurance riding, you will have to use a bit to comply with the rules but there is no reason why you cannot ride your pony in a bitless bridle at home.

A hackamore, as it is usually known, can give you just as much control as a conventional bridle and the horse or pony can be as well balanced as a top dressage horse. It can also be good for your riding, as you have to rely on legs, seat and balance instead of relying on your hands (as most of us do at least some of the time!).

If possible, borrow or buy the type of bitless bridle that is usually called an English hackamore. The German kind favoured by top show jumpers is more refined but potentially very severe – which is fine as long as you are sure you can ride as well as John Whitaker.

Practise in an enclosed area before you venture outdoors, to give both you and the pony a chance to get used to it. Once he is going nicely, you can introduce a mild bit again if you want to *as well* as the hackamore (fit a sliphead to your bridle to take the bit). Fasten a second pair of reins to the bit

Some ponies are easier to ride in a pelham than a snaffle, especially for jumping. This pony is wearing a vulcanite pelham, used with one rein and pelham roundings, and a running martingale

and use the same technique as described for riding off a noseband.

In theory, all of this should help you to decide what sort of bit might be best for your pony. In practice (because ponies are not exactly great students of theory), he may still find all sorts of ways to evade you. If so, see if one of the following sections has the answer to your problem: head shaking, leaning on the bit, opening mouth, strong.

Bolting

True bolting is one of the most frightening things a rider can experience but, luckily, it is pretty rare. A lot of people will say that a horse bolts when, in fact, it simply becomes strong and goes faster than they would like – if this is your problem, refer to the 'strong' section.

When a pony bolts, it is usually through fear. The problem is that it is in such a blind panic that the normal methods of controlling a strong or pulling pony have little effect. Basic instincts, such as self-preservation, can, unfortunately, be forgotten; all the pony wants to do is flee from whatever frightened it and it will not necessarily take any notice of hazards such as traffic or fences.

It is very difficult to plan evasive action while you are being carted at 90 miles an hour by a panicking pony. It is also very easy for someone else to tell you to try not to panic yourself, but it is true that the more you can keep your wits about you, the better your chances are of coming to a halt undamaged.

Your one aim must be to persuade the pony to stop or at least slow down. Leaning on the reins and pulling with all your might will only give him something to lean on – you have to make a distinct pull and give. Put one hand on the neck in front of the withers to give you a support and pull and give on the other rein in time with the pony's stride. Some bolters actually respond better if you drop the contact altogether so that they do not feel that you are trying to make them face the danger they so desperately want to get away from, but to do this takes some nerve on the rider's part.

Use your voice – not to scream for help or say your prayers, but to use whatever command you employ while lungeing or schooling to get him to slow down. Try to use the same tone of voice as you would then (it might sound as if this is asking the impossible but it is surprising how calm you can make yourself be in moments of crisis. By all means have hysterics later, but wait until the danger has passed!)

Just before this book was written, one of the authors was riding a four year old at his first show when something frightened him. He bolted across a field, taking a 1.2 m (4 ft) post and rail fence in his stride, and was heading for a main road. She dropped the reins altogether and said 'Whoa', in the same tone that had been used for long-reining and early schooling – and the horse stopped.

The standard advice for stopping a bolter is to turn him into a ploughed field, which is fine if you happen to have one handy. If the pony bolts in an open area, you can try turning him as long as you have the room to do so. He will be going faster than you ever thought possible, so your first turns will have to be wide and sweeping: this is not an occasion for 20 m circles!

If you can turn successfully once, you should be able to make gradually decreasing circles. Keep talking to the pony and giving and taking the reins until you can feel that his brain is back between his ears and you can come to a halt.

A pony who bolts in a one-off panic is one thing. If you can work out what caused it, you should be able to take evasive action. Get experienced help in accustoming him to whatever frightened him, whether it was a tractor or a herd of pigs. Do not try to cure the fear on your own; no matter how brave you are, the chances are that you will not be able to forget how frightening it was to be bolted with and will tense up at a potential hazard.

Check what you are feeding him in case you have literally blown his mind. Is he getting too much hard feed at too high an energy level? If he seems stressed or nervous, it could be worth trying a calming herbal supplement.

It is always a good idea to play safe and have a bolter checked by the vet. Ponies run away from pain, and so defective eyesight, a sore mouth or an injured back may be at the root of the problem.

The pony who bolts habitually is dangerous. He should be sent to an experienced professional who has been told exactly what the problem is and is prepared to take the risk of reschooling him. If this does not work, then, unfortunately, the only responsible action is to have him put down before he kills somebody.

Bucking

The occasional buck because a pony feels well or gets excited is very different from the serious variety, where the pony bucks as a habit. With the first kind, tell him off, shorten your reins, ride him forwards and make a note to give him more work and/or cut his feed if he is being generally a bit silly.

If bucking becomes a habit, look for the cause. Is something hurting him

Hitting a pony who bucks may have the desired effect – or it may simply produce a more spectacular effort

or is it a behavioural problem – for instance, does his saddle pinch or does he always buck when you canter in company?

It is much harder for a pony to buck when he is going forwards to start with, so if you feel one coming on, kick him on. The front end has to go down before the back end can come up but the pony will raise his head before he lowers it, so keep your rein contact as you push him on with your legs.

A standing martingale can help because it stops the pony from raising his head too high to prepare for the buck and gives you a neckstrap to hold on to. The standard advice is that a standing martingale should fit into the pony's gullet, but in this instance it may need to be very slightly shorter. It needs to be tight enough to prevent him from getting his head above the angle of control but not so tight that it is actually strapping it down.

You may find that you have a better chance of staying on the pony who bucks if you ride with slightly shorter stirrup leathers than normal. If he puts you on the ground regularly, ask a good adult rider to ride him for you for a while. Do not worry about their weight being too much for him – ponies can take more weight in relation to their size than horses, and it might help to make him realise the error of his ways.

If he bucks because he gets excited, you have to try the theory of familiarity breeding contempt. For instance, the pony who bucks when asked to canter in company should be ridden with one other quiet pony, first in front, then alongside and then behind until he starts to accept it.

Those who buck because they get excited about jumping usually try to deposit you as they land. Go back to trotting poles, turning away from them when he tries to rush and trying all the tactics in the jumping section. As he settles and you can build up to small jumps, remember that you must land and send him forward straightaway.

Hitting the pony who bucks will either have the desired effect or will provoke him into making a greater effort! Some will immediately come to their senses and keep all four feet on the ground but others will produce a more spectacular buck every time the stick makes contact with their sides.

Timing is vital. You must hit the pony as he bucks, not when he has had a rodeo session and comes to a halt feeling very pleased with himself. If you are sure you can stick with him – or can find an adult who can – then a good whack every time he bucks can put him off the idea.

Canter Problems

It is quite common for ponies to prefer cantering on one leg rather than the other. Check that you are giving the right aids and not inadvertently putting him off balance by leaning to one side.

As with any transition from one gait to another, you need to prepare the pony in advance by warning him that you are about to ask him to do something different. The way to do this is through a half-halt, or series of half-halts. Ride him forwards then close your fingers and sit up straight as if you want him to slow down. As soon as he does so, open your fingers and close your legs round him so that he goes forwards.

This 'pause' brings the pony off his forehand and puts him in balance ready to listen to your next instruction – in this case, to canter. Ask for canter in a corner or on a circle, rather than on a straight line at first, as he will find it easier.

To canter on the left rein, bend him slightly to the left and use your left leg on the girth. If, at the same time, you move your right leg back so that it is slightly behind the girth, it will help to stop his quarters swinging out. Look in the direction you are going and allow enough with your hands to let him go forwards from one gait to the next.

The pony who trots faster and faster rather than cantering is on his forehand. Practise transitions from halt to walk, walk to trot and down again, and use lots of half-halts to rebalance him. When you ask for canter, make your aids clear and definite.

Young ponies have to learn to canter with a rider on their back, which interferes with their natural balance. Be patient and do not be too worried if he runs into canter at first – make it easier for him by keeping your weight out of the saddle. As he gradually finds it easier, you can begin to sit lightly in the saddle.

With the pony who does not know how to canter or is reluctant to go forwards from trot, do not be too worried about getting the correct strike-off at first. It is a minor detail compared with actually moving up from one gear to another!

With a young pony, ask for canter going into a corner and then canter on down the long side of your schooling area. Your weight should be off his back – it is often helpful to ride with your stirrups slightly shorter than normal. He may manage just a few strides before flopping back into trot, which does not matter. As he progresses, he will manage to canter for longer periods.

If you are brave enough and the pony seems quiet enough (or if you do not have any other option!) you can teach him to canter in the field. Try to canter alongside a safe fence or hedge, which will give him some support, and pick level ground if possible. If a gentle slope is inevitable, canter uphill, never downhill at first – it is too difficult for him to maintain his balance if he is going downhill at speed and he may find himself unable to stop.

The pony who is reluctant to canter may improve if he has a cantering companion. The companion must be totally reliable and controllable. You want him to maintain a steady pace just in front, not gallop off into the distance if the reluctant pony decides he will have a go after all.

A pony who is quite happy to canter as long as he can choose which leg to lead with, needs transitions and half-halts as before, but there are also a few other tricks you can try.

If, for instance, he does not want to canter on the left rein, trot a circle on the right rein and then change the rein to make a figure of eight. As you circle left, ask for left canter. If you have prepared him properly, with the correct bend, you should get the correct strike-off.

Another exercise that often works is to put a small cross-pole fence three quarters of the way along the diagonal in your schooling area. Approach it in trot and give the aids for canter as the pony takes off – more often than not he will land and canter on with the correct leg leading.

Ponies are agile and clever and often a lot harder to ride than much bigger horses. If you have a pony who can wiggle better than a worm and insists on cantering the way he wants to, whatever you try, then a few lessons with a good instructor who is used to dealing with ponies can be the best answer.

Eating when Ridden

Few things are more annoying than the pony who snatches the reins out of your hands and puts his head down to graze as soon as you get on to grass. A strong rider can prevent this by anticipating when it is going to happen and riding him forwards but this does not work if your legs are not strong enough. There are also a lot of very clever ponies who know exactly when they can get away with this behaviour and when they cannot and only try it on when they know they are in with a good chance.

The answer is to fit a pair of grass reins, which can be made from baler twine. These are fastened to the bit rings and run up through the browband on each side to the D-rings on the saddle. They should be long enough so that they do not interfere with the pony's head carriage when he is being ridden, but short enough so that he cannot get his head down to eat. Some people fasten them directly from the bit to the saddle but passing them through the browband means there is no risk of them getting tangled up with the ordinary reins. Try not to use them when jumping but if you find you have to, do make sure that the pony can stretch his head and neck without them interfering.

Excitable in Company

A lot of otherwise sensible ponies get excited when ridden in company and the blame can usually be laid at the door of a young owner (not necessarily you, you will be pleased to know). Unfortunately, some children think it looks good to be seen on a pony who is leaping and dancing about and, instead of trying to calm it down, encourage this behaviour.

You need time, patience and help from a friend with a quiet pony to sort this one out. Most ponies get excited when they are ridden behind others, so, if you can, avoid going out in large groups while the 'rehabilitation programme' is in progress. Ride out on your own or with one other pony if you can – both the other pony and his rider should be quiet and sensible!

Start off by keeping your pony in front. Ride him quietly and sympathetically and do not carry a stick. Try to keep your rides calm – even boring. Do plenty of walking and encourage him to settle down. It may be tempting to have a good canter at your favourite places, but stick to walk so that there is no chance of the pony getting excited.

When he is settled and confident in front, ask your friend gradually to ride up alongside you. Let your pony stay slightly in front so that he does not think he is going to race, and keep riding quietly and talking to him. As he starts to settle – and it will not happen overnight – you can introduce short periods of trot. As he becomes more relaxed, the escort pony can very gradually move forwards until the excitable one is walking quietly behind him. It is a case of going step by step until the pony relaxes and even becomes slightly bored.

If your pony is a natural livewire, make sure you are not giving him too much to eat. Keep him out as much as possible (preferably day and night) and work him off grass in spring and summer. He will need extra food in autumn and winter, when the grass loses its food value, but you may find that plenty of good hay is enough.

Head in the Air

The pony who carries his head too high all the time is usually tense through the back and uncomfortable to ride. Jumping can be even worse because he will be hollow and flat.

A lot of ponies that go with their heads in the air are ewe-necked. If this is your pony's natural conformation, you will have to accept that you will never be able to get an 'ideal' head carriage and way of going because the pony is physically incapable of it. However, if carrying his head too high has created a ewe neck by building up muscle underneath, you may be able to change his head carriage and his shape over time.

The pony who carries his head too high all the time is usually an uncomfortable ride

You cannot persuade or force a pony to lower his head by pulling on the reins – this will only create more resistance. Instead, you have to get him to work from behind so that he comes round and down because he is in balance.

As always, once you have made sure that he is not uncomfortable in his mouth or back, it comes down to schooling. Ride lots of circles, pushing him out on a widening spiral with your inside leg, then spiral back in again by pushing him in with your outside leg.

As his head comes down, keep a light contact that allows you to feel his mouth but does not restrict him in any way. If you are riding in a snaffle, a drop noseband may encourage him to lower his head because it gives slight poll pressure. Make sure the noseband is set high enough not to restrict his breathing.

A pelham often encourages a pony to lower his head but it is important to use enough leg to keep him going forwards – otherwise there is a danger that you will simply winch in the front end and the pony's back end will still be trailing out behind.

There are many schooling aids or gadgets designed to help with problems such as this but they should only be used under expert supervision. In an ideal world, they would not be needed at all but, unfortunately, the real world is rather different. Fitted and used correctly on a *temporary* basis, many schooling aids can help to persuade a horse or pony that it is more comfort-able to go in an acceptable way.

There is no such thing as a 'magic wand' which will transform a pony which goes badly into a well-schooled animal overnight. Gadgets can help but it is vital to rule out all other possible causes, such as back problems and discomfort from ill-fitting tack, before introducing them.

Draw reins are the commonest training aid, but their potential drawback is that it is too easy to pull the pony's head in without using enough leg. Many riders also fail to reward the pony, by 'giving' on the draw reins as soon as he lowers his head, and so defeat the object they seek. Draw reins can be positively dangerous if the pony tries to rear and the rider does not give them immediately. It is all too easy to pull the pony over backwards in this situation.

One gadget that helps with some ponies is a correctly fitted Market Harborough. This looks like a running martingale but has clips on the ends instead of rings. It is used together with special reins with small D-rings sewn on to them. The clips go through the bit rings and fasten on to the D-rings on the reins.

Unlike draw-reins, a Market Harborough is worked by the pony, not the rider, which, in many cases, makes it preferable. When he raises his head too high, the pulley action puts pressure on the bit, and when he lowers it again the pressure stops. When it is fitted for the first time, fit it slightly loosely to start with until the pony gets used to its action.

The Abbot-Davies balancing rein is another device that may be frowned on by purists but it can make the difference between a pony learning that it is more comfortable to go nicely and one that is being an uncontrolled thug. Again, it should only be used under the supervision of someone who understands what is supposed to be achieved and how to achieve it.

Lungeing the pony in a chambon can also be effective, but it is important that the chambon is introduced properly and that the person lungeing the pony keeps him working forwards from behind but not rushing. The chambon – which should only be used on the lunge, *never* for riding – comprises a headpiece with rings and a second part which starts off like a martingale and splits into two straps with clips on the end. When it is first introduced, the clips are attached to the rings on the headpiece, putting pressure on the poll to persuade the pony to lower his head. As he gets used to it, the straps are put through the headpiece rings and then clip on to the bit. It needs to be adjusted so that it only comes into action if the pony raises his head above a certain point – not so that it is forcing his head down.

Head Shaking/Tossing

True head shaking, where the pony jerks his head in a peculiar flicking motion, is a veterinary problem rather than a behavioural one and is usually thought to be caused by some sort of allergy (see next section).

The pony who tosses his head while being ridden, tilts it to one side or shakes it without the characteristic flick of the allergy sufferer, is usually uncomfortable or in pain. Obvious causes are sharp teeth, ear mites, badly fitting tack or rough riding. Ask your vet to check his ears and teeth (unless you prefer to use a specialist horse dentist for the latter) and make sure your tack is not to blame.

Ponies have sensitive ears, and many object if the browband even touches their base. If it actually pinches, you cannot blame them for trying to get away from it.

Your saddle could also be to blame. If it is pinching or causing pressure points, the pony may throw his head about in a vain attempt to find a more comfortable position.

If everything seems fine and you still have problems, bad riding is probably to blame. The good news is that it is not necessarily you that is at fault; the bad news is that ponies can take a long time to accept that their new rider is not going to balance on their teeth in the way their old one did.

In bad cases, head tossing becomes a habit. The only answer is to fit a mild bit (a mullen mouth vulcanite snaffle or a plastic Nathe bit is often helpful) and a standing martingale. The martingale is for your protection, not the pony's: at least you will not get banged on the nose when he throws up his head.

Try to ride with a light but constant contact, using your legs to push him up into your hand. As the pony gains confidence, he should gradually adopt a steadier head carriage but be prepared for it to take time.

Another approach that often works is to ride the pony in a bitless bridle for a while. See the section on bitting difficulties and follow the plan of campaign outlined there.

Jogging

Jogging is an infuriating habit. Perhaps the second best ways of trying to cure it are not to ride the pony when you have had a bad day (or you will find it even more infuriating than usual) and to buy yourself a sheepskin seat saver, so that you can at least be as comfortable as possible! The first essential is to check that the pony is comfortable. Is his saddle pinching or is he uncomfortable in his mouth?

Jogging usually starts because the pony is excited and/or is trying to keep up with a bigger horse. In some ways you cannot really blame him. It is a bit like a little child who is holding his mother's hand and has to jog trot to keep up with her.

Your aim is to persuade the pony to walk in regular four-time, so either ride on your own or with another pony that has a similar length of stride. Stay as calm and relaxed as possible because any tension will be picked up by the pony and as soon as he gets tense he will start to jog again.

Your legs should be round his body, in contact with his sides; you often see children on jogging ponies sitting right back in the saddle with their legs stuck forwards. They think that if they keep their legs off the pony, he will slow down, but accepting the leg is an essential part of basic training.

Another key part of the equation is working out how much contact to take and this varies from pony to pony. Some settle if you take quite a firm contact, whereas others are better on a much looser rein. The only way to find out which technique will work with your own pony is by trial and error.

Never hit a pony for jogging, no matter how much it annoys you – you will only make things worse. Use your voice to calm him down. Also, although it may sound silly, check the rhythm of your own breathing. Holding your breath or taking quick, snatchy breaths will create tension in you and therefore in the pony. Taking long, regular breaths will have a calming effect.

If your pony only jogs on the way home, it sometimes helps to turn him round again as soon as he starts. When he settles, turn for home again, and so on. Tactics like this can take some time, so warn anxious parents and be prepared for a long ride.

In fact, long rides are often a very good idea. Many successful endurance horses and ponies are reformed hooligans who only settled when they were given a lot of slow work to occupy their minds.

If jogging is part of a pony's generally fizzy temperament, keep him out day and night and check that he is not getting too much hard feed. You may have to accept that he will always jog when he is excited but you ought to be able to improve things.

Jumping

Jumping problems can be divided into three main groups – ponies who do not want to jump, ponies who rush their fences and ponies who take a dislike to a particular kind of fence.

All ponies can be trained to jump to some extent but some have more talent and enthusiasm for it than others. If you want to jump a 1 m (3 ft 3 in) course and your pony's limit is 84 cm (2 ft 9 in), you will either have to lower your sights or find another pony!

Whatever your problem, it is essential to have someone experienced with you when you try to solve it. Often a few lessons with a good instructor are the answer but if that is not possible, ask an experienced adult to help. For a start, you need someone to move poles about for you – and if the worst happens and you fall off, at least there is someone there to make sure you are all right and catch the pony!

REFUSING

Ponies refuse for all sorts of reasons. Common ones are overfacing (asking the pony to jump a fence that is too difficult), presenting him at it badly (so he is in the wrong place to jump) and jumping when ground conditions are bad so that he is unsure of his footing. You can also do so much jumping that the pony gets sick of it and simply says, 'I've had enough.'

A refusal is much more of a definite 'No' than a run out and means going back to basics. First, are you sure that the pony isn't in discomfort from badly fitting tack, a sore back or whatever?

Second, could your riding be to blame? If you catch him in the mouth every time he takes off, or ride him at a fence so half-heartedly that he does not know what he is supposed to do, you can hardly blame him for stopping.

If none of the above can possibly apply and the pony is simply being naughty, hit him down beside the girth and, if the fence is small enough, make him go over it from a standstill. If it is of a size that makes that impossible, hit him and present him at it again.

Do not go miles away and gallop the pony into it in the hope that speed will get you over. Approach the jump straight on, not at an angle, in a controlled, bouncy pace with plenty of impulsion (remembering that impulsion means controlled energy, not speed).

Remember that you should sit fairly upright as you come in to a fence and keep your legs round the pony to tell him to go forwards. If you lean forwards in what is often called 'jumping position' on your approach, you are in no position to influence the pony. You should only go forwards from the hips when the pony takes off; as he lands, you should come back to your more upright position so that you can ride forwards to the next fence. If necessary (and as long as you are sure you can take your hand off the reins and keep him straight) give him a smack about three strides out as you approach – not as you take off. Always use your stick on the girth, not on the shoulder.

If the pony has three refusals in a competition, you will be eliminated. If this happens, try to jump him over a fence that you have already cleared before leaving the arena, so that he does not get the idea that if he stops he will not have to jump any more.

Refusing means going back to the drawing board, with the help of someone experienced who can watch both of you. If you have problems while schooling, perhaps because the pony gets his striding wrong at a double, get your expert to check that your distances are correct for your pony's length of stride and also lower the fences so that he can manage easily. This should restore his confidence and you can then gradually build up again.

Generally speaking, the smaller the pony, the shorter his length of stride and the shorter the distance needed between fences. As a guideline, for a 13.2hh–14hh pony, one non-jumping stride between two upright fences will be between 6 and 7 m (20–23 ft) and two non-jumping strides will be

Trotting poles help to settle a pony into a rhythm. They also encourage him to stretch his head and neck forwards and look where he is going

between 9 and 10 m (30–33 ft). These distances are for an approach in canter.

The pony who decides he wants nothing to do with jumping in any shape or form should be allowed a few weeks' break. Hack him out, school on the flat and let him do something different. You may well find that while he does not relish the idea of jumping poles, he is happy to pop over small logs when given a lead by another pony. Make sure the logs are small enough for him to step over if necessary.

When he has had a break, introduce him to jumping again by using poles on the ground. Scatter them around your schooling area and walk and then trot over them, concentrating on keeping your rhythm.

Then introduce trotting poles set about 91 cm–1.3 m (3–4½ ft) apart, depending on the pony's size and length of stride, starting with two and building up to five or six if the pony enjoys them. Some people will tell you that you should never have less than three trotting poles in case the pony tries to jump two, but we have never known this to happen and do not know anyone who has!

By now the pony should be happy about trotting over them, so put a pole between a pair of jump wings or stands and walk over it, then trot. Forget about the wings: this is just another pole. If, at any time, you get problems, stay calm and keep asking the pony to go forwards.

Leave it at that for the first session. Next time, trot over your poles as before and then put one pole on the ground 1.8–2.4 m (6–8 ft) in front of another pole between two wings. By now the pony should be relaxed about the whole thing, so raise *one* end of the pole between the wings by 15 cm (6 in). All that will happen is that he will take a bigger trot stride or make a small jump over it.

Pat him and get your helper to add another pole so that you now have a small cross pole. The height should be adjusted so that the centre of the cross is about 30 cm (1 ft) off the ground. Approach in trot with your legs round his sides, keeping a good rhythm. This is not so much a jump as a canter stride: the pony should trot in, hop over the cross pole and land in canter. Let him canter on for a few strides, then go forwards to trot.

Once you have established that jumping is not frightening or uncomfortable, you can build up gradually with the help of small grids. The idea of grids is that the distances between each fence are such that the pony arrives in the right place to take off, which gives him confidence. It is therefore vital that you have an instructor or helper who knows the correct distances and can adjust them slightly, if necessary, to suit a particularly long- or short-striding pony.

Sometimes ponies dislike particular types of fences, such as fillers or oil drums. Start by building a small upright (single pole) fence and use the fillers as wings. As the pony gets used to them, gradually bring them closer in so that he is jumping the pole between the fillers. Keep bringing them in until, eventually, he is so used to the fillers that he jumps them without spooking.

Small plastic drums, positioned so that they cannot roll, are also useful for introducing spooky ponies to solid fences. Start with an upright pole 46–61 cm (18–24 in) high, with another pole lying on the ground about 15 cm (6 in) in front of it (which is easier for the pony to jump than a single pole). Put a drum next to each wing so that the pony jumps between them. Gradually add one more at a time on each side until you have a solid fence.

Ditches are another common bogey. The best solution is to find somewhere where you can dig your own tiny one – 30 cm (1 ft) is wide enough to start with – so that the pony can step over it. Build a tiny fence above it, about 30 cm (1 ft) high, to encourage the pony and help to make him realise that he has to get to the other side.

If necessary, take a lead from another pony at first but always ensure that yours ends up by going over it alone. Make sure that you look ahead on your approach, not down at the ditch. As the pony grows in confidence, jump the ditch on its own. The take-off and landing must be firm, not slippery; if he cannot get his footing, he will not feel confident.

Always jump on reasonable going; if it is slippery or hard, it is not surprising if the pony opts out. If you intend to compete on going that may be a bit harder or wetter than is ideal, ask your farrier's advice about using studs. However, studs should not be looked on as a means of jumping on unsuitable going – if it is really hard or slippery, do not jump at all!

If your pony is reluctant to go through water, see the final entry in this section.

RUNNING OUT

The pony who runs out to one side or the other does so because his rider lets him. Check your approach: it must be positive but not fast and you should approach the fence straight. If you ride at it from one side to the other, it is hardly surprising if the pony decides that the easiest option is to go round.

In general, you have more control if you approach in a bouncy trot rather than canter, because you have more time to sort yourself out. Keep your fences low, about 46–61 cm (18–24 in) high. A pony can easily jump much higher than this from trot but it is sensible to stay low while you are having problems. A bit with cheekpieces, such as a Fulmer or full-cheek snaffle, often helps to keep the pony straight.

JUMPING TO ONE SIDE

You should aim to meet each fence straight and in the middle (except when you are so confident that you can tackle fences on an angle to save time in a jump-off). Some ponies hang to one side or jump at a slight angle, which can cause problems when you get two or three fences in a row. By the time you get to the last one, your angle of approach could be carrying you out to the wing.

Check that you are sitting straight and that you approach in a straight line, aiming for the centre of the fence. If you lean to one side, you will affect the

V-poles encourage a pony to jump the centre of the fence, rather than hang to one side

pony's balance. This is also a common cause of knockdowns, as he will then probably drop one foreleg lower than the other.

Cross poles, or a vertical behind a cross pole, encourage the pony to jump straight as his (and your) eye will be drawn to the centre of the cross pole as you approach. If the problem persists when you move on to uprights or small spreads, use guide poles to help.

There are two ways of doing this. The first is to lay poles on the ground on the approach, so that you ride along a 'channel'. If this does not work, use V-poles on the fence. Build a small upright and rest two poles on top to form a V; the pony will jump between these. At first, there should be a wide gap between them, which can be narrowed gradually as the pony realises what is expected of him.

RUSHING

The pony who always tries to jump as fast as possible has either been hust-led into his fences by a previous rider or is worried by jumping and wants to get it over with as quickly as possible. Contrary to popular belief, rushing into fences is not a sign that the pony loves jumping but, rather, that he is worried about it.

Go back to poles scattered on the ground, walking and then trotting over them and circling away as soon as the pony starts to rush. Once he has settled, build up to a line of three trotting poles. If he tries to rush through them, approach the first pole on a circle so that you trot over it and circle away between the first and second poles. Then go over two poles and circle away between the second and third.

Keep the pony thinking. When he has reached the stage of waiting for you to tell him where to go, trot quietly through the three in a row, then immediately go back to circling over one or two poles. This quiet repetition will soon help him to relax.

Eventually you will be able to introduce a pole or line of poles followed by a 46 cm (18 in) cross pole 1.8–2.4 m (6–8 ft) away from the last pole (the distance depends on your pony's length of stride). Always approach in trot. If the pony starts to rush, circle away – this is one of the rare occasions when you should deliberately turn away from a fence.

As your confidence increases, you can add more fences. Gridwork such as this is the best way to help a pony to jump confidently and in rhythm. As long as your distances are correct, he will meet each fence right – so make sure you have help from someone who can assess your pony's stride and adjust the poles accordingly.

Kicking Out

Any pony is likely to kick out if he is startled by something – such as a dog chasing him – or if another pony barges into him. However, a pony who kicks out if others invade what he considers to be his personal space can cause an accident.

Putting a red ribbon on his tail is the accepted signal to other riders that the pony is known to kick. This should warn them to keep their distance but it does not absolve you from trying to cure the habit.

You should also make sure that you have third party insurance to cover any damage the pony may do. This may sound pessimistic and with any luck it will not be needed – but if he kicks out and damages a car or, even worse, hurts someone, you could be left with a hefty bill and a guilty conscience. Third party insurance is included in British Horse Society membership.

Attempting to reform a kicker is usually a job for a professional trainer. The pony should be ridden by an experienced adult in the company of another rider of the same description on a quiet pony or horse. The escort rider must be able to get close enough for the kicker to threaten but stay far enough away to keep out of trouble.

When the pony threatens to kick, the rider should hit it behind the girth three or four times and also use his or her voice to make it doubly clear that the pony had better think again. This is one occasion when one slap is not enough. The pony must realise that kicking hurts him most, not other people and ponies.

Even if the habit seems to be cured, the owner of this sort of pony should never be complacent. Always try to keep yourself out of trouble and warn other riders to keep their distance.

Leaning on the Bit

Ponies lean on the bit because they are unbalanced or lack schooling. In both cases, they are on their forehand and trying to rely on their riders to hold them up rather than working from behind.

The answer is schooling – lots of transitions and half-halts. Make sure you are sitting straight and are not letting the pony pull you forwards.

Your choice of bit can make a big difference too. If you are using a 'fixed' bit, such as an eggbutt or full-cheek snaffle, swap it for a loose ring one. A loose ring, French link snaffle is often very effective.

Although it is theoretically a 'fixed' mouthpiece, a pelham or Kimblewick can also have the desired effect. The curb action, coupled with correct riding, makes the pony back off and rebalance himself. Purists and Grand Prix dressage riders may not agree, but this book is not intended for either!

Mounting, Difficulty with

As part of their early training, all ponies should be taught to stand still while the rider gets on. If yours walks off as soon as you put a foot in the stirrup (or as soon as you have both feet off the ground and are not in a position to do much about it), you need to check that he is not in discomfort from back problems and/or a badly fitting saddle, and then go back to basics.

If he is simply eager to get going, the problem is bad manners. However, in a lot of cases, ponies walk off or swing away from the rider because they associate someone getting on with discomfort – a toe in the ribs from a clumsy rider, or the saddle being pulled over as the rider heaves himself up.

When practical, it is a good idea to use a mounting block or to ask someone to give you a leg up because this stops you from pulling the saddle over. A lot of people pull themselves up by the cantle and, eventually, this could twist the tree. If you have to mount from the ground and find it

All ponies should be taught to stand while the rider gets on

difficult, perhaps because you have short legs or are not particularly agile, let the stirrup down a few holes and adjust it to your normal length again when you are up.

It is much easier to solve mounting problems if you have a helper who can stand by the pony's head. He should hold the bridle cheekpiece, not the reins – they belong in your hands.

Keep the reins short enough to indicate to the pony that you want him to stand. Make sure they are the same length. If one is much shorter than the other you may pull the pony off balance if he does try to move off, and he could then trip and fall. If he is used to being toed in the ribs and retaliates by trying to bite you as you get on, your helper should be able to stop him; if you have to manage on your own, you may have to shorten the right rein very slightly.

A few ponies wait until you are in the saddle and then swing round to bite at your foot. If yours has this delightful habit, stick your toe out so that it catches him before he gets you – he will soon decided that this is not a good idea.

Once you have got on, get off again and repeat the process. This is a problem that cannot be cured in five minutes: it takes practice, so arrange a short session every day for a week or however long it takes.

Movement, Injuries Caused by

A young and unbalanced pony, or one who does not move straight, may injure his limbs by knocking one against the other. Nothing can improve poor movement that is caused by bad conformation, but a young pony who knocks himself because he gets his legs in a muddle will improve as he muscles up and becomes more balanced.

In both cases, you need to do all you can to protect him. Your farrier will advise you whether he can shape the shoes to minimise the risk of injury, and the pony should also wear protective boots.

The most useful ones are brushing boots and overreach boots. Brushing boots (designed, not surprisingly, for the pony who brushes or knocks one leg against the other) cover the cannon bone and fetlock.

Overreach boots protect the pony who slices into the heel of a front foot with the front toe of a hind one. This can cause a nasty injury that takes a long time to heal. There are two kinds of overreach boot. One looks like a rubber bell and the other is made up of detachable plastic 'leaves' threaded on a strap which buckles round the coronet.

There have been cases of ponies treading on the back of the rubber bell kind and tripping themselves up, which should not happen with the leaf variety – the leaves break off if necessary and can be replaced. Rubber overreach boots are safe as long as they are not too long. If necessary, trim a piece off the bottom. The only trouble with the leaf boots is that they flap and make a noise that can be extremely irritating!

Napping

Napping varies in severity, from the pony who digs his heels in and says he does not want to go any further, thank you, to one who stands up, whips round, runs backwards at 90 miles an hour and does everything he can think of to avoid going where you want him to. Some ponies nap on a hack, some refuse to leave the yard and others nap at the entrance to a show ring.

It is a horrible habit but it can be cured by a strong, experienced adult rider. Just as important, it can often be prevented. Nearly every pony tries it on at some stage; a lot of youngsters suddenly decide they would rather not leave the yard today or go past something spooky and do the pony equivalent of sticking out their tongues and saying, 'What are you going to do about it, then?'

The answer is that you give them a good wallop and concentrate on riding them forwards. A pony can only nap if he is not going forwards, so if yours shows this tendency, keep him active and working.

Do not stop to admire the view or chat with a friend and *never* return home by the same route as you went out. Riding up the road, turning round and riding back again is an open invitation to a pony to decide that he would rather turn round a bit earlier.

With youngsters, or ponies who have never shown signs of napping before but decide to try it on with a new owner, it is a habit that can usually be nipped in the bud. However, it takes confidence and strong riding, so if you are not absolutely sure you can cope, enlist the help of someone who can.

If you are unlucky enough to get stuck with a confirmed napper, the task is a lot harder. The best way of making sure you do not get caught is to test for the tendency when you try a pony – ride him in front of his escort going out of the yard and away from home. When you get back, make sure he is happy to go on past his own gate: a nappy pony will usually dig his heels in or mess about.

However, while that advice may help next time you buy a pony, it will not sort out the one you already have. And though you may wish you could get

Sponsored rides are a good way of encouraging nappy or lazy ponies to go forwards, as long as the pony is fit enough to cope with the distance

rid of him, he will be difficult to sell (except at a loss to someone who knows about the problem and is prepared to take it on).

There are various tactics that an experienced rider can use with a nappy pony. The first is to ride him carrying a schooling whip and wearing spurs and to use both at the first signs of resistance.

The second is to play a waiting game, which is boring and time consuming. If the pony comes to a halt, let him stand there, facing the way *you* want to go. Eventually – and this could take a long time – he will decide to move on. This is where you refuse to let him do so – he must go forward when you want him to, not when he decides to. Some ponies are so surprised at this that it soon works wonders.

One tactic with the nappy pony is to play a waiting game

You can also try disorientating him. Steer him round in the tightest of circles, using strong legs and an open rein so that he is virtually circling on the spot. Then straighten up without warning and immediately use your whip hard to send him on. The biggest danger is that you will make yourself feel as dizzy as the pony, so look up and ahead rather than down as you turn him.

A pony who runs backwards or refuses to leave the yard should be met by an opposing force, such as a helper who is handy with a lunge whip. Do pick someone who can be guaranteed to wallop the pony not the rider!

Throwing a bucket of cold water up his backside can also shock him into going forwards. If he naps on leaving the yard, make sure you have someone acting as lookout – you do not want him to shoot forwards and out of the gate in front of a car.

A pony who tries to spin round can be the most annoying and dangerous of all, especially if he couples this with rearing when you try to turn him back. As he will inevitably put his head up to spin round, you need to make sure that he keeps it in a controllable position: a standing martingale will help.

The key is to ride him forwards into your hands, not to pull his head down. Most ponies try to spin round the same way every time – usually to the left – so be aware of this and ride forwards into your contact. Riding a nappy pony on a loose rein is tantamount to giving him an open invitation.

The pony who naps when he is asked to go in front of another or to hack out alone is quite common. All youngsters should be taught to go out alone when necessary. Start by taking him out with a schoolmaster a few times, asking him to go behind, alongside and, eventually, in front of the other horse.

Nothing is worse than a pony who will only go with his nose immediately behind another one, so always vary your position. If you meet something spooky, the schoolmaster can quietly come forwards to give him a lead past it without him realising.

Once the young pony is hacking out and taking the lead confidently, it is time for him to go solo. Choose a short ride that he has done before and insist that he keeps going forwards: never stop to 'let him have a look at something'. Working alone should be part of his education and he should accept from the start that he goes where you tell him to.

Ponies who are always ridden in company, such as riding school ones, are often (and not surprisingly) reluctant to go out alone. If you acquire one of these, enlist an escort, to start with, who can ride in front of, then alongside and eventually behind you.

The escort should gradually drop back until your pony is way out in front. Keep him going forwards, not lagging back to wait for the other and, once his leader position is established, take him on a short, familiar hack by himself.

Some ponies nap at shows when asked to enter the ring. This may be because you have been standing around in the collecting ring with a crowd of other ponies and suddenly ask him to leave them. Do not put yourself in this position. Get a helper to tell the steward that you are ready to go in; if you explain that the pony may nap, most officials should understand that you do not want to stand about. Keep him moving and, when your turn comes, go forwards smartly.

If the entrance is blocked by people and ponies standing around, ask the steward to clear a gangway for you. You must, of course, always be careful of your own and other people's safety. You do not want to let your pony get away with bad behaviour but, on the other hand, it is unfair and potentially dangerous to have a confrontation where someone might get hurt. If necessary, get a quiet, confident helper to lead him into the ring (holding the cheekpiece, not the reins) and to step back quietly as soon as you are in.

A pony who is plain naughty needs a good sorting out by an experienced rider but you need to pick your time and place. Try to find a small show with sympathetic organisers and a clear-round jumping ring or something similar.

With the steward's help, find a time when no one is waiting to go in and insist that the pony goes into the ring with the help of lungeing whip and strong riding. If you call his bluff a few times, he will usually give in.

Naughty at Shows

Going to shows can be a mind-blowing experience for young or inexperienced ponies. It can be a bit of a shock when your quiet pony does a Jekyll and Hyde conversion and turns into an excitable little monster who seems unable to keep his brain between his ears and all four legs on the ground.

You need to get him used to the atmosphere before you start competing. Make sure that he is not hyped up by too much hard food – if you can keep him out all the time so that he is as relaxed as possible, so much the better.

Pick a small local show and get there nice and early before the hustle and bustle builds up and the loudspeakers go into action. Allow plenty of time for the journey and use travelling bandages, not boots.

The reason for choosing bandages is that you can tape over the ends for maximum security (making sure that the tape is no tighter than the bandage) and leave them on while you first work the pony. That way, you will not be struggling to take off travelling boots and put on brushing ones while the pony dances around.

It is a good idea to put his bridle on in the trailer rather than waiting until he is unloaded. This will give you more control.

If the pony comes off the trailer with his eyes popping out on stalks, find a quiet corner where you will not get in anyone's way and put him on the lunge until he starts to settle. Maximum control is essential, so, provided the lunger is experienced and skilled, the pony should be lunged off the bit, not off a lunge cavesson. To lunge on the left rein, put the lunge rein through the left snaffle ring, pass it behind the chin and clip it to the right ring. To lunge on the right rein, thread the rein through the right bit ring and clip it to the left one.

When he has settled enough for you to be confident that you are not going to get on an unexploded bomb, go back to your quiet area and ride some circles and transitions on both reins. Keep him going forwards and listening to you but do not force anything – both you and the pony should stay relaxed.

Then walk him round the showground and let him look at everything. Keep out of the way of competitors who are warming up, but, as the pony relaxes, ask a little more of him. Make him stand while you chat to a friend and then ask him to leave the other ponies and trot a couple of circles by himself. He will probably find all the excitement tiring, so do not use him as a grandstand seat. After an hour or two's riding round, he will be ready to go home.

When he has been to one or two shows like this, he will start to get used to all the distractions and you can look forward to your first competition.

Open Mouth

A lot of people complain that their ponies resist by opening their mouths – and they then make the situation worse by strapping them shut so tightly that the poor animals can hardly move their jaws, let alone accept the bit.

Do not expect your pony to keep his mouth clamped shut all the time (after all, do you?). At the same time, if he persists in opening his mouth so wide that he evades the bit, you have to do something about it.

The first step is to check that he is not trying to get away from pain or discomfort. If his teeth are sharp or he has wolf teeth that are interfering with the action of the bit, or you are using too much hand when you ride, he will open his mouth to try to ease himself. Solve the problem and he will stop resisting.

If none of the above is to blame and he has simply realised that this is an effective way to resist, a change of tack will help. In many cases, a broad, snug cavesson noseband – dropped down a hole if necessary – will work just as well as a noseband with some kind of drop strap.

A Flash noseband looks like a cavesson noseband with a narrower strap stitched to the centre at the front, which fastens below the bit. It is perhaps the mildest form of drop noseband, but only works if the cavesson part is broad enough to stay in place; too many are so narrow that the drop strap drags them down in front, making them ineffective and untidy.

The drop noseband is a 'classic' piece of tack, which, for some reason, went out of fashion. It is now becoming popular again and rightly so as long as it is properly adjusted. A drop acts on the front of the nose, in the curb groove and also gives a little poll pressure, so it helps to persuade the pony to lower his head. It must be fitted high enough so that the front does not rest on the soft part of the muzzle and restrict the pony's breathing.

Never use a drop noseband with a curb bit or a standing martingale. The action of curb chain and noseband together would be confused and using a standing martingale would interfere with the pony's breathing.

The Grakle or figure of eight noseband was invented for, and named after, a hard-pulling Grand National winner. It can be effective on ponies who resist by crossing their jaw and setting themselves against your hand.

Whatever type of noseband you use, remember that you are using it to prevent the pony from opening his mouth *too far*, not trying to strap it shut.

Rearing

Rearing is a frightening problem that should only be dealt with by an expert. First ask your vet to check that the pony is not protesting because of pain in his mouth or back, and then find a professional to assess him and, with luck, sort him out.

A pony often rears because his rider asks him to go forwards but does not allow with the hands. When this happens, he has nowhere to go but up. Rearing can also be part of a nappy pony's repertoire of evasions. If you are unlucky enough to be sitting on one who goes vertical, it is vital to keep your weight forwards – if you lean back and hang on the pony's mouth, you will put him even more off balance and he may well go over backwards.

Keep forwards and grab the mane. As soon as the pony lands, send him forwards without restricting him with your hands. He cannot rear if he is going forwards.

Unfortunately, rearing is a vice that is rarely one hundred per cent curable, unless there is a physical problem behind it. If the pony has learned how effective this resistance (or just the threat of it) is, he will nearly always retain the tendency.

Confirmed rearers are not safe and should not be sold to anyone other than a professional who is aware of the problem and is prepared to try to cure it. The only other alternative is to have the pony put down.

Shying and Spooking

All ponies shy or spook at some time, usually either because they are feeling a bit too well (and therefore silly) or because they are startled by something, such as a bird flying out of the hedge. Sometimes they will shy at 'ghosts' – it is amazing how many pony-eating dragons live under drain covers!

From the rider's point of view, shying is an annoying and occasionally unseating habit. Ponies are not usually as prone to shying as horses. A sharp Thoroughbred can be walking along perfectly quietly one second and at the other side of the road the next, having given you no warning at all!

If the shying coincides with the flush of new spring grass, an increase in food and/or less exercise than normal, you generally need to look no further. Increase the work and cut the food and the pony's brain should soon be back between his ears.

If shying is not coupled with a general impression that the pony is feeling a little 'over the top', ask the vet to check his eyes and his hearing. It is amazing how many 'confirmed shyers' cannot see or hear properly.

If everything is all right physically, you have a behavioural problem to cope with. Some ponies are naturally spookier than others but you have to decide whether he is lacking in confidence (common with young ponies or those who have not had a good general education) or just plain naughty.

Take him on some rides with a quiet, well-behaved pony. Concentrate on riding him forwards and making him pay attention: do not slop along on a loose rein, letting him goggle at everything.

Basic schooling is vital. If the pony understands how to move away from the leg, you can use this to ride him past anything potentially spooky.

Most ponies raise their heads before they shy, so fitting a standing martingale helps. Some are much more relaxed and controllable in a vulcanite pelham than a snaffle: the mouthpiece is a mild one and the poll pressure helps to persuade the pony to keep his head in an acceptable position. Ride him forwards, from the leg into the hand, and you should be able to work him in a round outline – which will also mean that he is more controllable.

If you can keep him going forwards between hand and leg, he will find it much harder to shy. Anything that helps you to achieve that, such as a change in tack, is worth trying; it might not be strictly orthodox but being orthodox does not always solve problems.

Once the pony is riding quietly with his escort and is confident enough to take the lead without spooking at every waving leaf, take him on a familiar hack by himself. If he starts shying, ride strongly, using your voice to urge him forwards, but try to stay relaxed. This might sound rather like trying to pat your head and tub your stomach at the same time but it can be done. What usually happens is that you get so exasperated by the pony's behaviour that it lends you an added determination.

However tempting it might seem, never lose your temper. If you thrash a pony for shying, you merely confirm his belief that there really is something to be frightened of.

If the pony shies when you are schooling, the best approach is often to ignore it but to insist that he works. For instance, if he shies every time you go past a pole in the corner, give it a fairly wide berth but insist that he still goes forward in a round outline. Make him bend and do lots of transitions and changes of direction – in other words, give him plenty of other things to think about. Every time you pass the pole, you will be able to get a little closer. Eventually, the pony will ignore it without you having had to force the issue.

A strong (which does not mean rough) rider is essential for dealing with shying or spooky ponies, so, if necessary, ask a lightweight adult to help.

Strong

A pony who is strong and either pulls or takes more of a hold than you would like – so that you may sometimes be moving on in a higher gear than you had in mind – is very different from the pony who bolts (see the section on bolting). Strong ponies can be managed: bolters are dangerous.

You can often guess when a pony will be a strong ride by looking at his confirmation. If he has a thick neck, with more muscle below than on top, the chances are that he will go with his head in the air. Calluses on either side of the mouth are another giveaway!

It is best to avoid buying ponies like this but if you already own one you are stuck with doing something about it. Check that his teeth and mouth are all right, because pain from sharp teeth or mouth ulcers will make a pony pull more, not less.

Is he stabled for too long and getting too much to eat? Turn him out as much as possible and make sure that any extra hard feed he needs (if he actually does need any) is non-heating.

Some people say that their ponies are strong when, in fact, they are simply on the forehand and lean on the bit. Schooling is the answer – lots of transitions and half-halts to get the pony off his forehand and working from behind.

A change of tack can do the trick with a pony who is genuinely strong. If you particularly wish to ride in a snaffle, forget the inevitable thick eggbutt which most ponies are ridden in – these make it easy for them to lean. A thinner, loose ring, single jointed or French link snaffle, coupled with a drop or Grakle noseband, will give you more control. A running martingale may also help.

Strong ponies usually pull or take hold when they are jumping or hacking in company. In these situations, you are often best switching to a pelham, which has the effect of making the pony 'back off' and bring his hocks underneath him, thus lightening the forehand.

Tongue over the Bit

When a pony puts his tongue over the bit, or draws it right back, there is no 'cushion' between the mouthpiece and the bars of his mouth so he is actually making himself uncomfortable. Unfortunately, ponies with this habit do not necessarily realise this, which can make life somewhat difficult.

Young ponies often try to put their tongues over the bit when they are first broken, as part of their attempt to get rid of the strange thing in their mouth. It is therefore vital to make bitting as comfortable and untraumatic as possible. Make sure the bit fits and perhaps smear it with molasses or honey to make the idea more palatable.

Once the habit is established it is hard to break but it can be done. First, and most important, make sure that the pony does not have sharp teeth or mouth or tongue ulcers and check that his bit is the right size and is sitting high enough in the mouth.

Many people use bits that are too big. Then, if the mouthpiece is a jointed one, it will hang lower in the mouth than it should and this will encourage the pony to put his tongue over it. You should not be able to get any more than the width of an adult's little finger between the cheekpiece and the pony's lips on each side. It must be high enough at least to wrinkle the lips on each side. If necessary, fasten it a hole higher to make it more difficult for the pony to get his tongue over.

Use either a cavesson noseband, fastened tightly, or a drop noseband. If the pony cannot open his mouth very wide, it is harder for him to get his tongue over.

Some ponies dislike pressure on their tongues, so trying a different bit might help. A French link snaffle reduces tongue pressure and a pelham or Kimblewick with a low port allows room for the tongue.

Look at the shape of your pony's mouth and tongue. If he has a short mouth, he will not have room for a thick mouthpiece. If he has a fleshy tongue, he will be much more comfortable with a French link snaffle than with a single jointed one.

Snaffles with roller mouthpieces work in some cases. The pony plays with the rollers rather than drawing back his tongue and eventually realises that he is much more comfortable with his tongue lying underneath the bit.

A rubber tongue port or metal tongue grid on a separate sliphead is another idea worth trying. A rubber tongue port fastens over the centre of the bit and although it will not stop the pony from drawing back his tongue, it should stop him from getting it over the bit. The trouble is that some ponies manage to push them to one side and carry on as before!

Traffic-shy

Most ponies soon become used to traffic if they are introduced to it in the proper way, by being ridden out with a reliable escort who accepts most things in his stride. The right rider is important too. Traffic training takes a firm but sympathetic jockey who can ride the pony forwards but stay relaxed, thus giving him confidence.

Problems usually arise either because a vicious circle builds up between rider and pony – the rider tenses up and grabs at the pony's mouth if he shows signs of nervousness, thus reinforcing the pony's fear – or because the pony is unfortunate enough to have been involved in an accident or a near miss.

Accidents are all too common. The latest statistics in Britain show that there are at least eight road accidents a day involving horses and the real figures are probably much higher. Ponies and traffic do not mix well, so it always makes sense to pick the quietest routes possible, away from busy roads. Even then a traffic-shy pony is dangerous as you are bound to meet local and farm traffic even on the quietest roads.

Always make sure that motorists can see you; a brown pony and a rider in a green jacket will blend into the hedge. Fluorescent and reflective clothing mean that you will be spotted in time for the motorist to slow down (with luck) and give you a wide berth.

Traffic problems should *only* be dealt with by experienced professionals. The best method is for the nervous pony to be ridden out with a reliable escort on his right side and to be positioned with his head alongside the escort horse's flank, just behind the rider's leg so that the escort horse acts as a shield. If a potential hazard approaches, talk to the pony, sing to him – do anything to stop yourself tensing up. Keep your legs round him and push him up to a definite, but not restricting, rein contact.

With the pony and escort in this position, the danger vehicle will be past almost before he realises it is there. Once the pony has regained his confidence in this position, drop back slightly. As his confidence grows, ride him alongside the escort and then gradually edge in front. Eventually, you should be able to ride the pony in front of the escort horse.

Traffic rehabilitation is a matter of time and patience. A professional who knows what he or she is doing can often give the pony confidence in six to eight weeks and it is then up to the rider to build on that basis.

Water, Reluctance to go Through

You might realise that the water jump or large puddle you are asking your pony to go through is perfectly safe but, unless he has been taught that he can and must trust you, he will be reluctant to go anywhere where he cannot see that the footing is safe.

If your pony is reluctant to go through water, start by encouraging him to follow a reliable companion through puddles with a safe footing

As soon as there are some respectable puddles, find an obliging escort – a pony with no fear of water who can be guaranteed to splash straight through. The puddle needs to be wide enough so that he *has* to go through: little ones are too easy to sidestep. Let the escort give you a lead and tuck your pony in as close behind as is safe. Do not let him turn away but keep insisting that he goes forwards. Be prepared for him to try to jump it the first couple of times.

Once he is walking through happily behind another horse, get the escort to wait on the far side and then ride towards him. The final step is for your pony to go through first.

Alternatively, see if you can hire a cross-country course with a small water splash and follow the same tactics as above. Check the footing first by walking through yourself. The last thing you want is for your pony to find a hole in the ground and slip.

Do not accept any well-meaning helper's offer to lead your pony through. What usually happens is that the pony throws up its head and socks itself in the teeth or dances about and lands on the helper's toes.

Some ponies love water but others are always suspicious and need strong riding. As with any argument, it is important to finish what you start. If you give up and go home it will be twice as difficult next time.

Some ponies love water, but others are always suspicious of it

SECTION 3

Common Health Problems

No matter how tough and hardy your pony is, there are bound to be times when he becomes ill or hurts himself. Some hardly ever need to be seen by a vet except for preventive measures, such as vaccinations, while others have the knack of attracting trouble like a magnet. If there is a single flint to stand on in the field, this sort of pony will find it – preferably the day before an important event.

Safeguarding your pony's health is important, so you need to recognise when something might be wrong. This does not mean just spotting when he is lame, it means noticing when he seems off-colour or when his habits or behaviour are different from normal.

To recognise when something is wrong, you have to know what is right or normal. The trouble is that it is too easy to become a horsy hypochondriac. You pick up a book that tells you that a healthy animal has a shiny coat, look at your hairy beast (or what you can see of him under the mud) and worry that he is sickening for something.

You have to work out what is 'normal' for your pony – for instance, if he is so laid back that he would not bat an eyelid if a bomb exploded under his nose, he is not necessarily ill just because he prefers conserving his energy to being energetic. However, if he becomes listless and uninterested in the food that is normally his main focus in life, the warning bells should sound.

There are some useful guidelines as to what signifies good health. The basics are temperature, pulse, breathing rate, consistency of droppings and colour of urine, lack of appetite and changes in behaviour.

The normal temperature is 38°C (100.5°F), although it can vary half a degree either way depending on the time of day and the individual animal – foals, for instance, have a slightly higher temperature than adult ponies. Anything outside those limits will probably be accompanied by other signs of ill health and this means that you should definitely call your vet.

Taking a pony's temperature is not difficult, although it does take practice. Practise when he is well and you have plenty of time, rather than when you have an emergency.

Unfortunately, you cannot ask a pony to 'open wide' and put the thermometer under his tongue in your best Florence Nightingale manner. You have to go to the other end and take the rectal temperature. Use a plastic-coated digital thermometer, which is safer to use and easier to read than the old-fashioned glass variety.

Most ponies are pretty obliging, although the odd one will jiggle about and test your dexterity. Lubricate the thermometer with petroleum jelly and get someone to hold the pony: a bridle gives more control. Standing just behind and to one side, hold his tail to one side and insert the thermometer using a twisting sort of gentle push. Leave it there for one minute (or until a digital thermometer bleeps) and *keep hold of it all the time* so that it does not disappear inside or fall out if the pony decides to pass droppings!

The normal heart rate for a horse or pony at rest is between 35 and 42 beats per minute; it will be higher in young animals, especially foals. The heart rate obviously increases with exercise (as yours does if, for instance, you run up the road) but if it goes up and stays up, this is a sign of distress.

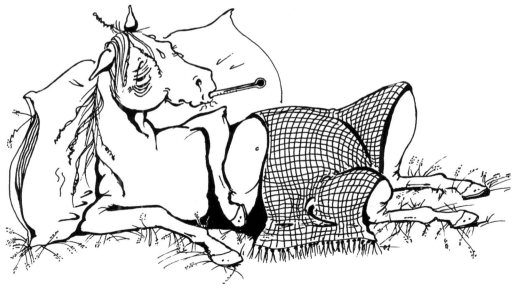

Unfortunately you cannot expect a pony to 'open wide'...

There are two ways of checking the heart rate. One is to use a stethoscope (basic ones can be bought quite cheaply) behind the pony's left elbow. The other is to feel for the pulse in the facial artery on the inside edge of the lower jaw.

It is also useful to be able to take the digital pulse in the fetlock. If this is stronger than normal – and you will have to know what 'normal' feels like to work this out – it is often a sign that something is wrong in the foot; for instance, if the pony has a punctured sole and infection starts building up, the digital pulse will inevitably be stronger. The best person to show you how to feel for this is your farrier or vet. If you find it difficult, it is often because you are pressing down too hard.

The normal breathing rate for a pony at rest is eight to twelve breaths per minute. The easiest way to gauge this is to stand behind and slightly to one side and count each rise and fall of the flanks as one breath.

The consistency of the droppings depends on what the pony is eating, so if there is a sudden flush of spring grass do not be surprised if they become looser than normal (and be aware of the risk of laminitis). Urine should be clear to pale yellow and the pony should not be struggling to stale (pass water). A noticeably darker colour, or tinges of blood, mean that you should ring your vet. Other warning signs to watch out for are a discharge from the nostrils, swollen glands or a habitual cough.

So, when should you call the vet? The simple answer is any time you are not absolutely sure you can cope by yourself and any time the pony seems distressed.

Everyone knows that vets' bills can leave a large hole in your budget but if you take out insurance with a good company against veterinary fees, you know that you 'only' have the insurance premium and the first £75–95 or so of any claim to pay. Bills are the same whether the patient is a £500 pony or a £50,000 competition horse – and when you think that a colic operation could cost £2,000 plus, insurance really is common sense for the average owner.

There are times when speed is of the essence and the vet must be called immediately. Colic, or the suspicion of it, is one of them; arterial bleeding (bright red, spurting blood) is another.

You should also consult your vet if you think a wound might need stitching or if any lameness that does not have an obvious cause, such as injury, persists after three or four days' rest. The injury may, of course, need veterinary treatment in any case.

Basic preventive measures, such as worming, vaccination against flu and tetanus and teeth rasping, are vital measures to help to keep your pony

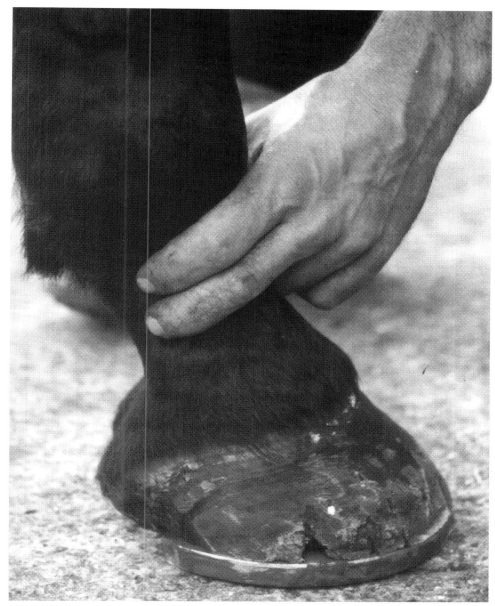

Feeling for the digital pulse. This pony had badly cracked feet and weak heels when photographed but her feet improved tremendously with the attention of a skilled farrier

healthy. Your vet will advise you on programmes for the first two; teeth rasping should be carried out at least once a year, depending on the advice of your vet or equine dentist.

Finally, make up two first-aid kits – one to keep at home and the other to take to shows. You can bet your bottom dollar that if you only have one at home, the pony will cut himself as soon as you go somewhere else.

If you have to drive to a livery yard or field to get to him, keep your 'home kit' in the car along with one for humans. Mark the pony one with a blue cross to distinguish it from the white cross human kind; it also means that you know which one to look in for the aspirin when the pony causes yet another headache!

The basics for a main first-aid kit are:
  skin swabs (useful for cleaning around the wound and mean that you do not need water)
  antiseptic wound powder (preferably one which contains fly repellent)
  antiseptic spray
  non-stick wound dressing
  Gamgee tissue
  Animalintex poultice
  crepe bandage
  three self-adhesive bandages
  stable bandages
  scissors with rounded ends
  thermometer (plastic-coated digital ones are safer and easier to read)
  cotton wool
  two large, unopened packs of cotton wool to form a Robert Jones splint in the case of a suspected fractured limb

Your travelling first-aid kit should include:
  skin swabs
  antiseptic wound powder
  wound dressing
  Gamgee
  crepe bandage
  self-adhesive bandage
  cotton wool
  cotton wool packs for Robert Jones splint
  stable bandages
  scissors

Ready made first-aid kits are available but it is usually cheaper to make up your own.

Some people are amazingly cool and efficient at dealing with health emergencies, whereas others go to pieces at the first sign of blood. Whatever happens, try to keep calm and assess the damage.

If you need the vet, you can at least tell him or her what to expect and also answer any questions. If you are not sure whether or not you need the vet, play safe – he will not mind a false alarm. It is better than letting a situation get worse when prompt treatment was needed.

Most vets and their staff are pretty good at assessing via a phone call when a visit is necessary. Never be worried that you will look stupid: the vet has spent five years in training and many more gaining practical experience, which is rather different from reading books and keeping your fingers crossed that you are doing the right thing!

Remember that a pony who is in pain may be difficult to handle. Try to keep calm and take every precaution for your own safety. Even treating minor injuries such as small cuts can cause a major accident to the handler if the pony is not handled correctly; stand in the wrong place while you are cleaning a cut hind leg and you could get a nasty kick.

This section is intended to provide basic information and simple guidelines. It cannot be emphasised too strongly that if you are at all worried or are not sure what to do, you should call your vet.

Azoturia

Azoturia, or exertional rhabdomyolysis, used to be called Monday morning disease – because it was common in work horses who had Sunday off but were kept on full feed. Mild cases may be little more than a slight stiffness of the muscles in the quarters and loins, but severe ones – when the pony seems unable to move and is obviously in distress – can be quite frightening to witness.

It used to be thought that giving too much food on a rest day was the only cause of azoturia, but vets now believe that there are many other reasons for it as well. An imbalance of mineral salts called electrolytes has recently been highlighted as a factor in many cases.

Azoturia can strike seemingly without warning. If it happens, try to move the pony as little as possible and get someone to call the vet. Throw a rug over his loins and quarters to try to keep him warm. If it strikes while you are out riding, use anything you can to keep him warm until the vet arrives or you can get a friend or parent with a box or trailer out to get him home.

The vet will give painkillers and perhaps intravenous electrolytes. He will also take a blood test to confirm that the problem is actually azoturia.

If it happens once, it may happen again – some ponies are more susceptible than others. Remember to omit hard feed if the pony is not being ridden (which you should always do in any case). You can always give the pony a handful of chaff and a few sliced apples or carrots to keep him happy.

Vets now recommend that any animal which has suffered an attack of azoturia should be given 25 g (1 oz) of common salt mixed in with his feed each day as a preventive measure.

Botflies

Botfly eggs – little yellow dots seen round the pony's legs in late summer – should be removed either with a hard dandy brush (if the pony does not object to this) or a special bot knife, which you can buy from most saddlers.

Do not leave them there in the hope that they will go away. They will, but only because the pony licks them off and they hatch into larvae in his mouth. They then move on to the stomach, where they cause damage.

Not all wormers are effective against bots, so use one that is at least twice a year as part of your worming programme. If you are not sure which products to use or when, ask your vet's advice.

Colic

Colic is not a disease but simply another word for abdominal pain. It always counts as an emergency – ring the vet as soon as you suspect that the pony might be suffering from it. If possible, take the pony's temperature so that you can report this to the vet. If this is difficult because the pony is throwing himself about in pain, your priority must be to get the vet to him as quickly as possible.

If treated promptly, colic can usually be dealt with. If it is left too long, however, the pony will be in great pain and may even die. The danger signs are sweating, restlessness, pawing the ground and/or a rise in temperature. The pony may turn his head to bite his flanks or kick at his belly in protest at the pain. In many cases, he will try to roll in an attempt to relieve it.

It used to be thought that it was important to keep the pony moving and to stop him rolling at all costs in case he twisted a gut. Modern thinking is that if a twist is going to happen, it will happen regardless, and that the safest thing to do is to get the pony into an area where he can do as little damage as possible to himself.

This may mean moving him from a stable, where he could injure himself or get cast, into a field. Play it by ear but do not try to move him by yourself. A pony who is in pain is not easy to handle.

The vet will give him a pain killer and a muscle relaxant, which, with luck, will do the trick. In some cases, surgery may be the only option. The success rate is much higher than it used to be, but the high cost (£2,000 is not unusual) is one of the best arguments you could have for veterinary fees insurance.

Worm damage is one of the commonest causes of colic. Even if you worm your pony religiously, previous owners may not have been so conscientious. Rain followed by a sudden flush of grass can also set it off – a greedy pony will stuff himself silly if he gets the chance, so restrict his grazing when necessary.

Corns

Corns are found under the heel of the shoe, usually in the front feet. They are areas of bruised sole which can only be seen when the farrier takes off the shoe; as he cuts carefully into the horn, you will see bruising.

The bruised sole will be cut away and the pony might need to rest for a day or two without his shoe on. Poulticing sometimes helps to relieve the pain and is essential if there is any infection.

Good shoeing at regular intervals is vital to prevent the recurrence of corns. Some ponies are prone to them and may need shoeing more often than usual and with wider shoes.

Coughing

Every pony gives an occasional cough but if it becomes habitual you know there is a problem and that you need to call the vet. If the pony seems listless or unwell and/or has a runny nose or swollen glands, the chances are that the cough is part of an infectious condition. (See Strangles.)

Even though it may be a case of shutting the door after the pony has bolted – because the problem may have already spread to others on the yard – it makes sense to isolate him if possible.

If he seems otherwise well in himself and the cough is a dry one, it is more likely to be a dust or spore allergy which may develop into COPD (chronic obstructive pulmonary disease, where the flow of air in the lungs is obstructed). The only answer, apart from drug treatment that your vet will advise you about, is a dust- and spore-free management regime.

The biggest culprits in this sort of case are dust and spores from hay and straw, so you will probably have to rethink your feed and bedding routines. The best management technique is actually the simplest – turn the pony out and keep him out, with rugs and extra feed, if necessary, in winter.

If you wish to, or have to, stable him at night, you will have to forget about using straw unless it is the vacuumed, virtually spore-free kind. Even then, some kinds are impregnated with disinfectant which makes many people cough and splutter when they put down new bales. If it does that to people, it is probably not doing a lot of good to the pony either.

Alternative beddings include dust-free shavings (be careful as not all shavings are dust-free), paper, hemp products or one of the rubber matting systems used alone or in conjunction with a suitable bedding. All have advantages and disadvantages, whether they be price, availability or difficulty of manure disposal, so you have to weigh up the pros and cons and decide which would work best for you.

Hay is an important part of most ponies' winter diet; some will be all right on best quality dry hay as long as they are kept out, but not all. Those who still cough, together with stabled ponies, will need either soaked hay, bagged forage or hay substitute.

Soaked hay is only beneficial if it is still wet while the pony eats it. Soaking 'sticks' the spores to the hay. As soon as it dries out you are back to square one (so always remove uneaten hay). It used to be the golden rule that hay had to be soaked for a least twelve hours but researchers now say that if you do this you soak out all the nutrients. A time of ten minutes to four hours is now recommended by many nutritionists.

So far so good. But what about when the water pipes freeze and soaking hay is impossible? Your options then include bagged forage, alfalfa products and high-fibre hay substitute cubes.

Bagged forage is more expensive but is consistent in quality. Ponies will need the lowest-nutrient type and, even then, you may feed less than with ordinary hay, so it will not keep the pony occupied for long. If you are feeding from a haynet, put the full net inside another one – the smaller holes mean (in theory) that it will take him longer to pull the hay through and therefore longer to eat it. It has to be said, however, that some ponies would rather destroy a haynet than eat more slowly!

Alfalfa products can be very useful. They usually keep the pony occupied longer than nuts or cubes, thus decreasing the risk of boredom if the pony has to be stabled for part of the time.

Cuts

Cuts often look much worse than they are. This may not seem much comfort when you go to catch your pony and he has blood running down his leg, but it may help you not to panic!

Having said that, wounds which are so small that they are easily overlooked can be very troublesome if they get infected. Puncture wounds (see separate section) are the worst of all; a tiny hole in, say, the sole of the foot can cause no end of trouble if not dealt with correctly.

The first thing to do when you find that your pony has injured himself is to assess just how bad the damage is. If you can move him easily to the stable yard, do so and work from there; if he is badly hurt, get someone to call the vet immediately while you try to control the bleeding.

Bright red, spurting blood means that an artery has been severed. This needs urgent specialist attention, but you will also need to control the bleeding until the vet arrives. Forget any idea of tourniquets, which are now regarded as potentially dangerous unless applied by a vet. If the wound is on a limb, put a non-adhesive dressing, topped by a clean cloth pad, over it and a pressure bandage on top.

If your pony is awkward enough to injure himself this badly elsewhere on the body, press your dressing and pad against the area from which the blood is spurting and hold it there firmly until help arrives. (It is at times like this that a mobile phone suddenly seems to be an essential part of your first-aid kit!)

All this, of course, presupposes that the accident has happened while your first-aid kit is within reach. If the worst happens and your pony cuts himself badly while you are out riding, your priorities are to control the bleeding and get the pony home (or get a vet out to him if that is not possible). This may mean improvising a pad and bandage, even if you have to knock on the nearest door and ask for help.

That is the worst scenario – thankfully, a rare one. Small cuts and grazes are much more common and are dealt with easily. They usually stop bleeding of their own accord and simply need cleaning and treating with an appropriate antibiotic ointment, powder or spray. Ask your vet which he recommends.

If the wound is more than about 2 cm (1 in) long or if it gapes open, it may need to be stitched. Never apply powders, sprays or creams to a wound if you think the vet needs to look at it: he will only have to clean off all the gunge before he can do anything. Clean the area gently with plain, clean water or, if possible, a dilute disinfectant solution – be careful not to make up the solution any stronger than the manufacturers' recommendations or it may do more harm than good.

The emphasis is on cleaning gently; water should be trickled on to the wound from above so that any dirt and foreign bodies are washed out. A cleaned-out worming syringe is useful for flushing out cuts and is sometimes easier to use than a hosepipe. If there are any large particles in the wound, such as splinters, remove them with a pair of tweezers.

As soon as you think you have removed the dirt, stop washing. If you carry on, so will the bleeding, as blood clots will not get a chance to form.

Left to his own devices, a pony will soon get a nice clean wound dirty again. The best way to prevent this is to cover it with a non-stick dressing with a bandage over the top until the wound is dry. Some places are more awkward to bandage than others, but one of the special self-adhesive bandages, which sticks to itself, makes the job easier.

It goes without saying that your pony should be protected against tetanus. If you are not sure about his vaccination programme, tell the vet so that he can give him an anti-tetanus shot.

Sometimes 'proud flesh' forms as a wound heals. This is fibrous tissue which forms a bump over the wound – ask your vet whether you need a preparation, such as copper sulphate cream, to 'burn' it back. If left, it will form a permanent blemish.

Fractures

A suspected fracture (broken bone) is a real emergency, so call the vet immediately. Fractures happen suddenly, usually to the limbs. They can be caused by anything from a fall to a kick from another horse and the pony will usually not be able to bear weight on the injured limb.

A fractured leg may look as if it is at a peculiar angle or there may be swelling. Try not to panic because modern treatment can save many ponies which, in the past, would have had to be put down.

Send someone for the vet and, if you have the means available, find an experienced person to put on a Robert Jones splint. This holds the leg still and should stop broken bones grating on each other until the vet arrives. It comprises one, or preferably two, large rolls of cotton wool wrapped round the leg and held in place with a bandage applied as tightly as possible.

Grass Sickness

Grass sickness is a disease of the central nervous system. As yet there is no definite known cause but it is potentially fatal and needs urgent – and specialist – veterinary attention. Sufferers are unwilling to swallow and are often reluctant to drink as well as to eat. They become dejected and can lose weight dramatically. In its acute form, it can kill a horse in 48 hours.

The good news is that many animals who are suffering from the slow, or chronic, form of grass sickness can be saved. The risk of the disease is highest between the beginning of April and the end of July, so be especially vigilant then for signs of loss of appetite, listlessness and weight loss.

The risk of the disease is also heightened when the mean daily temperature, during a ten-day period of dry weather, stays within a band of 7–11°C (45–52°F). A run of frosty mornings can also contribute to its occurrence.

Research has shown that horses and ponies aged between one and seven years, which are kept out all the time, are most at risk. You would obviously cause more problems than you would prevent by stabling your pony all the time, but be aware of the risk of grass sickness and call your vet if you have the slightest suspicion.

Head Shaking

Every pony shakes or tosses his head at some time, especially when he is bothered by flies. 'Proper' head shaking is very different: the pony gives a quick and abrupt shake of his head, sometimes striking out with a forefoot at the same time.

Causes can range from ear mites and teeth problems to allergies. Your vet will start by checking the obvious – that his ears and teeth are not causing him discomfort and that he does not have soreness in the saddle area, caused by badly fitting tack. If these investigations draw a blank and it seems that an allergy is to blame, finding a solution becomes more difficult. However, current research offers hope for the future.

Many head shakers are only affected during the spring and summer (which, of course, is the time of year when you are likely to want to do more with your pony). If you can narrow it down to a likely cause, you might be able to take evasive action.

Tiny midges which irritate the nostrils are thought to be a common cause of head shaking. Riding the pony in a 'nose net' – a fine net pouch which encloses the muzzle and is fastened to the noseband – may help. You can buy purpose-made ones or you can cut the end off a nylon stocking (as long as you do not mind the jokes about which bank you are going to rob). Sometimes, attaching a fly fringe to the noseband works.

Your vet will advise you about drug treatment. There is also an operation which basically involves desensitising the nostrils by severing nerves. This works in some cases but not in others.

Lameness

Insurance companies say that lameness is the commonest cause of claims for veterinary fees, so, by the law of averages, it is something you are bound to have to cope with one day! The first thing to do is to work out which foot or limb is causing the problem; if there is an obvious injury you have an equally obvious answer. If not, you need to see him trot up.

Most cases of lameness only show up in trot – a pony who is obviously lame in walk is very lame. Find a hard, level surface if possible and get someone to trot the pony towards and past you. He needs to be run up on a loose rein or rope so that his head can move naturally.

Lameness in front is easier to detect than lameness behind. The pony who is lame in front will often nod his head; how much depends on how painful he finds it to move. His head will drop when the sound leg comes to the ground and rise when the lame one takes the weight – the easiest way to remember this is to say that he 'sinks on the sound leg.'

It often takes a very experienced eye to identify lameness behind. Watch the pony being trotted away from you; he will raise his hindquarters on the lame side when that leg hits the ground, to try to avoid putting weight on it.

Life becomes more complicated if the pony is lame in both forelegs or both hind legs, as he will neither nod nor raise his quarters in the same way. Your only indication is a 'pottery' stride in front or a shorter one behind.

Most cases of lameness, however, are straightforward and easy to identify. You then need to see if there are any obvious causes, such as a stone lodged in the foot, or if you can feel heat or swelling anywhere in the affected limb.

Vets say that 90 per cent of lameness is centred in the foot, so if the limb feels and looks the same as its partner, the chances are that this is where your pony is affected. A stronger than usual digital pulse often points to the problem being the foot. If the farrier can come out to you reasonably quickly, you can ask him to take off the shoe and check for obvious causes, such as a punctured sole or corns (see appropriate sections).

This can be a tricky area, as a farrier is not a vet and vice versa. A farrier cannot diagnose or prescribe but farriers and vets work together and most vets will not mind if you have asked the farrier to eliminate obvious causes.

If there is no obvious cause of lameness, ring your vet. He may be able to spot something you cannot see, or he may ask you to box rest the pony for two or three days and then trot him up to see if he is still lame.

Laminitis

Laminitis is a painful condition, usually of the front feet only, which can literally cripple a pony. In its most acute form, it can lead to changes inside the foot that leave the pony in agony.

Signs and degrees of laminitis vary, but it should always receive veterinary attention. Some ponies may be lame or show pottery, shuffling strides, while others may show signs similar to colic: the pony may be sweating and blowing and will lie down to take the weight off his feet.

The old name for laminitis is fever in the feet and some people will tell you that there is no danger unless your pony's feet are warmer to the touch than you would expect. Ignore this advice because foot temperature is not an accurate guide.

What does help is learning to take the digital pulse (in the digital artery at the fetlock joint). If you know what this pulse normally feels like, you will be able to recognise when it is stronger – a useful danger sign. You should also be suspicious if you find that your pony is lying down more than normal or standing with his front legs propped forwards and his weight on his back ones.

Always ask your vet's advice if you suspect that your pony has laminitis because treatment stands a far better chance of success if it is started early. The vet will certainly want the pony brought off grass and he will also ask the farrier to trim the feet according to his instructions. Drug treatment, remedial shoes and X-rays may form part of the regime.

Many cases of laminitis can be caught in time and the pony restored to a normal, working life – as long as he is looked after very carefully. Prevention is a vital aspect because laminitis is not a 'one-off' condition that gets better and never returns: susceptible ponies are always susceptible.

The most important thing is to keep him off rich grass during the growing periods in spring and autumn. Do not forget that September can be as dangerous a month as April in this respect. One of the best ways of doing this

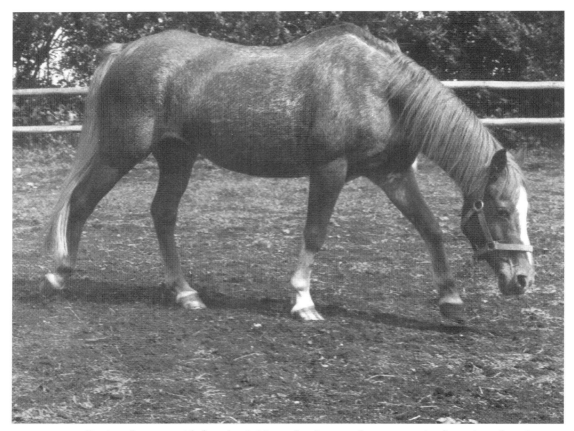

Ponies who are at risk from laminitis need to be turned out on restricted grazing when the grass is at its richest

is to set up a very small grazing area with electric fencing, turn a non-susceptible animal on to it first to graze it down, then turn your pony out when it is much less lush.

Lice

Lice are small, yellowish-white flecks in the coat that you might mistake for bits of scurf – the difference is that they move about! Horse lice do not affect humans but they are definitely unwelcome visitors because they make their pony host itchy and uncomfortable.

Lice will live in the coat all year round but you tend to notice them more in the winter months because they are more active in cold weather. They bite the skin and suck blood and cause such irritation that an affected pony will often rub himself raw to try to relieve the itching.

Your vet will advise you about products to use to get rid of lice. You will also need to check, and probably dust, other animals in the same field, as lice will spread from one pony to another.

Mud Fever and Rain Scald

Mud fever and rain scald are caused by a bacterium in the soil, which needs wet conditions in order to thrive. Mud fever is found on the lower legs, while rain scald usually affects the back and quarters.

White legs are usually more prone to mud fever than dark ones, perhaps because the skin is more sensitive. Like rain scald, mud fever shows as clumps of matted hair and scabs; the hair comes away in small clumps.

You need to clip away the hair on the affected leg and remove the scabs, either by picking them off and/or cleaning the area with an anti-bacterial shampoo every three days. Only pick off the scabs if they can be removed easily and, as the pony will be sore, be careful not to get kicked or stamped on.

Keep the leg area clean and dry and apply antibiotic ointment or whatever else your vet suggests. Once the mud fever has cleared up, use one of the good creams available which are designed to act as a barrier.

If the mud fever does not respond to treatment after a few days, you will need to get your vet to look at it. He will probably give the pony a course of antibiotics.

Rain scald generally looks less unpleasant than mud fever, as the scabbed areas are smaller. Remove the scabs and shampoo as before, dry thoroughly and repeat every three days until all the scabs have gone.

With both of these conditions, the important thing is to get rid of the scabs, which shield the bacteria underneath them.

Overreach

When a pony hits the back of his front foot with the toe of his back one, he overreaches. This can cut the heel of the front foot and because there is usually bruising as well, the wound is sometimes slow to heal.

Never ignore an overreach even if the pony is not lame. Clean it up and, if necessary, cover it with a non-stick dressing and bandage until it is dry. If any swelling starts in the lower limb, or if the wound is so large that it might need stitching, call your vet.

Punctured Sole

If a pony treads on a flint or nail, or grit works its way between the shoe and the foot, he may end up with a punctured sole. Dirt works its way in through what can often be a barely perceptible hole and infection sets in, resulting in a build-up of pus under the sole and a lame pony.

Your farrier or vet will cut into the sole to drain out the pus and you will have to poultice the foot to make sure all the pus comes out. The drainage hole should be plugged with antibiotic wound powder to stop more infection setting up.

Use an Animalintex poultice, applied according to the manufacturers' instructions, and hold it in place with self-adhesive bandage. You can buy special poultice boots but they are very expensive and some designs rub and cause more problems than they solve. Poulticing makes the area soft, so do not poultice for more than 48 hours.

Ringworm

Ringworm is one of the real nasties, a fungal infection that spreads quickly from horse to horse – and even from horse to person. Despite the name, it has nothing to do with worms and the telltale patches of crusty skin which characterise it are not necessarily round.

It is usually found in areas where the tack rests, particularly the saddle and girth region, although it can break out anywhere. The infected pony should be kept away from others and any horses he has been in contact with should be checked. The incubation period is about two months, so a pony may infect others before anyone knows he has ringworm.

Your vet will probably give you powders to put in his food and an anti-fungicidal washing mixture that may leave his coat dull but will help to kill off the ringworm. You also need to wash any tack, grooming equipment and rugs that have been in contact with him in the anti-fungicidal wash.

Ringworm is a very good reason for making sure that every pony has his own tack and equipment: sharing brushes can also lead to sharing skin infections.

Sarcoids

Not surprisingly, a lot of people get confused about the difference between warts and sarcoids. Warts are small growths that often crop up on the faces of young ponies; they disappear of their own accord and do not cause any problems. Sarcoids are much larger and often appear on the legs, chest, abdomen and groin.

If the sarcoid is on a stalk, tying a piece of cotton round it may result in the sarcoid 'dying' and dropping off. Alternative measures include ointment or conventional surgery or cryosurgery (freezing) which can only be carried out by your vet.

Homoeopathic remedies can have excellent results and at least one company markets an equine sarcoid remedy. Herbal remedies can also be effective in some cases. However, always consult your vet first – not because such treatments are in any way dangerous but because the pony may need other treatment as well.

Strangles

Strangles is a highly infectious respiratory infection which has some very unpleasant results. The pony will feel and look dejected and will usually have a thick nasal discharge, a high temperature and probably a cough.

Things get worse as the disease progresses and first the lymph glands under the jaw enlarge, then abscesses form. As these rupture, pus comes out through the skin.

It is important to isolate all actual or suspected strangles cases and to call the vet. He may give antibiotics and he may also want you to bathe the jaw with pads wrung out in hot water, to encourage the abscesses to come to a head and discharge their contents – unpleasant but necessary if the pony is to recover as quickly as possible.

Sweet Itch

About two per cent of ponies suffer from sweet itch. If yours is one of them, he will spend a lot of the summer rubbing his mane and tail to try to relieve the itching. Basically, it is an allergy to a type of biting midge and, like all allergies, it can be relieved but not cured.

If possible, bring the pony in during the late afternoon during summer and stable him overnight. Use plenty of fly repellent on him, round the clock, and hang fly papers in the stable out of his reach so that he cannot try to eat them!

In the past couple of years there have been new lotions and potions, said to be more effective and longer-lasting than the traditional benzyl benzoate: ask your vet's advice.

Tendon Sprains

Sprained tendons are not that common in ponies but they can happen. They are more of a risk in performance horses, which, of course, is no consolation if your pony lands awkwardly over a jump and suffers the same injury.

There are two tendons at risk: the superficial digital flexor tendon and the deep digital flexor tendon. Both run down the back of the leg.

Any sign of heat or swelling in the tendon area is a signal to apply cold treatment, put the pony on box rest and call the vet. There are some very sophisticated cold packs and 'frozen bandages' on the market, which are kept in the freezer in case of an emergency like this, but if you do not have one, bandage on a packet of frozen vegetables, such as peas, instead! The other alternative is cold hosing but this is not usually as effective.

Your vet may give a cortisone injection and will certainly want the pony to be rested. Rest offers the only hope of recovery – the amount of time the pony has to be off work varies according to the severity of the injury and can be anything from a few weeks to a year.

Thrush

If your pony has smelly feet, the chances are that he has thrush. The frog of the foot (or feet) becomes soft and in bad cases the pony will be lame.

Thrush is usually seen in stabled ponies rather than grass-kept ones because damp, dirty bedding encourages it to thrive – good stable hygiene is vital. Even grass-kept ponies can develop it, though, if their feet are not picked out regularly.

Your farrier will trim the frog and you can clean out the affected area with hydrogen peroxide solution. Use an old, clean wormer syringe to squirt it into all the nooks and crannies, then use antibiotic spray to clear the infection and to help to dry out the frog.

Warbles

Warble flies are much more common in cattle than in ponies but if one chooses your pony as a suitable host, he could end up with a sore back. The life cycle of the warble fly sounds like something out a horror film. The flies lay their eggs on the animal's legs and when the larvae hatch out they move under the skin to the animal's back.

In theory, they stay there until they hatch out through the skin, but in practice they often die before they are ready to hatch and then the vet has to open the area and clean it out. For some reason, the larvae seem to prefer to settle in the saddle area, so watch out for summertime lumps and ask your vet's advice if you suspect warble flies might be the cause.

Wolf Teeth

Some, but not all, ponies have wolf teeth – small pre-molar teeth with shallow roots. (Do not confuse them with the larger tushes in male horses.) They are found in both sexes and often cause discomfort because they are sited where the bit rests.

Some vets and horse dentists remove them as a matter of course, whereas others prefer to leave them alone unless they seem to be causing trouble. Because they are so small and shallow, their removal is quick and easy; the pony should not have a bit in his mouth for three or four days afterwards, to allow the area to heal.

Conclusion

It is likely that you picked up this book because you are having a problem – or problems – with your pony. Hopefully it has helped you realise that most problems can be solved with a mixture of time, patience, determination and technique.

You should also take comfort from the fact that you are not alone. Every time you are driven to distraction because your pony refuses to be caught/bucks/does not want to go in the trailer, remember that someone else is feeling equally annoyed because of a pony that hates being shod/shies/does not want to go through water.

Ponies are not machines, a fact which guarantees that keeping and riding them can be both fascinating and infuriating. Solving problems is part and parcel of owning a pony, and every time you take a step forwards you will increase your confidence and ability.

Keep calm, be as devious and determined as the pony if necessary and you will achieve your objectives in the end. You might even find some solutions that we have not thought of, if so, please let us know. With ponies and horses, you never stop learning!